Triumph Books and colophon are registered trademarks of
Random House, Inc.

Library of Congress Cataloging-in-Publication Data

Mikita, Stan.
  Forever a Blackhawk / Stan Mikita with Bob Verdi.
    p. cm.
  ISBN 978-1-60078-614-3
  1. Mikita, Stan. 2. Hockey players—United States—
Biography. 3. Chicago Blackhawks (Hockey team)—History.
I. Verdi, Bob. II. Title.
  GV848.5.M5V47 2011
  796.962092—dc23
  [B]
                              2011028477

This book is available in quantity at special discounts for your group or organization.
For further information, contact:

Triumph Books
  542 South Dearborn Street, Suite 750
  Chicago, Illinois 60605
  (312) 939-3330
  Fax (312) 663-3557
  www.triumphbooks.com

Printed in U.S.A.
ISBN: 978-1-60078-614-3
Design by Paul Petrowsky
Photos on p. xxii, 2, 4, 6, 10, 13, 14, 16, 19, 33, 36, 58, 140, 144, 151, 153, 154, 157, and 180 courtesy
of Stan Mikita; photos on p. iv, vi, viii, xiv, 1, 23, 60, 80, 85, 88, 95, 96, 103, 108, 113, 116, 120, 122,
126, 130, 131, 132, 136, 164, 169, 172, and 178 courtesy of Getty Images; photo on p. x courtesy of Matt
Vanderzalm; photos on p. xix, 26, 158, 163, and 182 courtesy of the Chicago Blackhawks; photos on p. 47,
48, 63, 74, 77, 78, 91, 92, 118, 129, 134, and 149 courtesy of The Louis Okmin Collection and Herb Kanter

FOREVER
A BLACKHAWK

Stan Mikita
with Bob Verdi

TRIUMPH
BOOKS

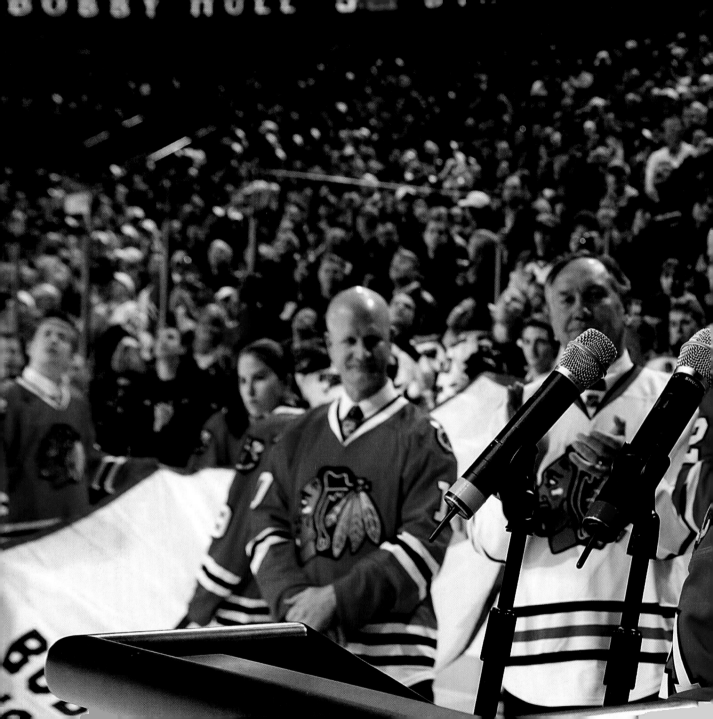

"I'd just as soon be remembered as an athlete who was part of the community. Chicago, after all, is my home."

—STAN MIKITA

CONTENTS

xvii INTRODUCTION *by Glenn Hall*

CHAPTER 1

FROM SOKOLČE TO ST. CATHARINES

3

CHAPTER 2

THE ROAD TO THE NHL

29

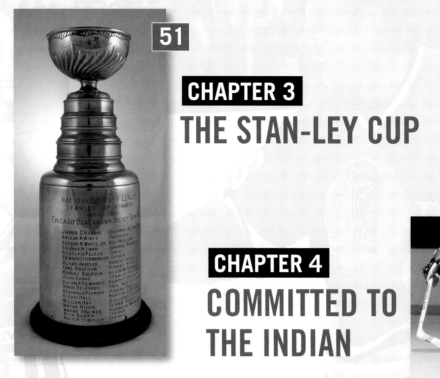

51

CHAPTER 3
THE STAN-LEY CUP

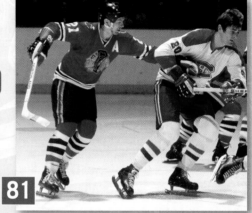

81

CHAPTER 4
COMMITTED TO THE INDIAN

139

CHAPTER 5
A FAMILY MAN

159

CHAPTER 6
HAPPILY EVER AFTER

INTRODUCTION
by Glenn Hall

I was about 10 years older than Stan Mikita when he joined us as a rookie with the Blackhawks, but we became friends quickly. I'm still about 10 years older than Stan, and we remain great friends. I don't know what it's like now, but in those days, your best friends were your teammates. When we came off a road trip, we would all go out together along with our wives, who were also close. Stan was single when he came up to the NHL, and my wife, Pauline, and I hit it off with him. He was a cocky little bugger, but if you had the kind of talent he had, you would be cocky and confident, too.

We all went through the same thing to make it to the NHL. We had to leave home early to refine our skills, and while we were playing hockey, we all got homesick. I can only imagine what it was like for Stan, who left home in another country at the age of eight and settled in Canada, not knowing a word of English. I think that contributed to his personality and to his hockey. He was tough and took no guff from anybody. There was no question he would be a star. When people describe him as the best hockey player, pound-for-pound,

Despite his rough style on the ice, he was great around people and a terrific teammate. There was no generation gap in our day. We didn't haze rookies beyond maybe making them carry our bags onto the trains once in a while. I don't know that Stan would have carried mine if I did ask, by the way. He said I taught him a lot, but I'm not sure he needed much teaching. During his early years, as we all know, he took a lot of penalties. The only thing I might have drilled into him was that if some guy on the other team ran him, he didn't have to get him back on the very next shift. We played 14 games against every other team. There was plenty of time to retaliate. Just file it away and pick your spot down the road. Stan gradually realized that he was more valuable to

Glenn Hall (fifth from left) won three Vezina Trophies and the Calder Memorial Trophy during his illustrious NHL career. He backstopped the Blackhawks to their Stanley Cup victory over Detroit in 1961 and was inducted into the Hockey Hall of Fame in 1975.

us on the ice than he was in the penalty box, and I think when he got married to Jill and started a family, he understood that he could be an even better player if he didn't talk back to referees and accumulate those misconducts. That's about the only change Stan ever made, as far as I can see.

He never acted like a superstar and he doesn't walk around like a Hall of Famer now. He was always down-to-earth, a solid person, and you can see in his children what a great job Stan and Jill have done as parents. Stan was never satisfied being mediocre, so he constantly worked to become better and more productive. Part of that involved being more disciplined. We all loved what we were doing, so much so that we would have probably played hockey for free. The owners would have liked that. We lived and breathed hockey. We might go to a movie as a group, and all of sudden, you look over and there's

Ab McDonald and Kenny Wharram and Stan talking hockey. Stan was a great student of the game, not that anyone could learn the instincts he had. The really special players always seem to have a vision of where the puck is going instead of where it is, and Stan was always a step ahead. Despite all the changes in hockey now, I have no doubt that he could have adapted to them in his day and been just as or even more productive.

I was honored to be the best man at Stan and Jill's wedding. I live a long way from Chicago now and I'm not too good about picking up the phone to stay in touch. But, after more than 50 years, I still feel the same way about Stan Mikita as I did when we were teammates. We never got tired of each other then, and we never get tired of each other now when we see each other. The only thing that's different is that we both get tired more often than we used to.

"I don't know where my aggression stemmed from, but it might have had something to do with feeling like an outsider for so long."

—STAN MIKITA

FROM SOKOLČE TO ST. CATHARINES

It might seem as though I was born on skates, but that is not the case. I was born in Sokolče , a small village in the eastern portion of what used to be Czechoslovakia, and I did not know that hockey even existed until I was eight years old. I watched some of the kids in the neighborhood play hockey on the nearby pond, but the game never really grabbed me. What did catch my attention were the skates that belonged to my brother Juraj, who we also called George. He was three years older than I was, so obviously his feet were not nearly the same size as mine. But his were the kind of skates you could sort of make fit, much like modern inline skates. So one day when he wasn't around, I put on his skates and more or less adjusted them until I felt comfortable, then headed off to the pond. I fell on my behind at least three times. I just did this by myself, with nobody supervising and nobody watching.

I didn't get caught until three days after I returned the skates. My mistake was that I had walked to and from the pond on the skates over gravel, and my brother noticed that the blades were a little rusty and dull. He asked me if I had "borrowed" them. Naturally, I said no. And naturally, Juraj said if I didn't tell him the truth, he would rough me up. So I admitted that I used

Me and my brother, Juraj

them for 20 minutes. And that was that. I had no interest in hockey, and even less interest in trying to steal those skates again and having my brother threaten me. The idea of people being able to glide along a hard ice surface intrigued me, but I postponed my interest in skating, and eventually hockey, for a long while.

What happened in between, now that's quite a story. For one, my name was Stanislav Gvoth. My father, Juraj (or George) Gvoth, worked as a maintenance man in a textile factory and my mother, Emilia, worked on our land, which wasn't much. She helped raise vegetables and potatoes. We lived in what I would call a bungalow consisting of two small rooms. Behind the house was a barn where we kept a cow, a horse, chicken, geese, and a couple of pigs. Indoor plumbing was only a rumor; when it came time to take a bath, Mom would have to get water from the pump outside, heat it up over a primitive wooden stove, then pour the water into a tub along with me. The notion that we were poor never occurred to me, nor did I know anything about politics. I vaguely remember World War II and how German soldiers came through our village. They would basically take over our bungalow for a few days while we moved to the barn. I recall them being nice to me, maybe because I was so young and so cute. They would assign me certain chores, like fetching food or soup from their mess hall nearby, and once in a while I would get some candy as a reward. They also let me go with them to the rifle range and pull a trigger. I would stand beside and behind a soldier when he fired. I felt the vibration through my whole body. What a recoil.

Meanwhile, Emilia discovered that the soldiers had lice. She went to the commanding officer, the captain or sergeant, and he actually listened. He took the two soldiers outside, started a fire, and threw all their clothes into it. Then our house guests took everything from the bungalow, furniture and mattresses included, and burned all of that. Then, I want to say it was the very next day, a big truck pulled up with all new stuff for us. Nice bed, new chairs. No more lice, and soon the soldiers were gone. We had a second wave of German soldiers who came into our village and billeted themselves in our homes. But the commanding officer of that group made sure to tell my mother that they would not be bringing any lice with them this time. I have to say that, in my limited recollection, we were treated well by the German soldiers. By the time I was five or so, World War II was over, but that didn't mean we were living in a free society. On the contrary.

I really didn't understand Communism until I escaped from it.

In 1948, we were visited by my aunt and uncle, Anna and Joe Mikita, who had left Czechoslovakia years before and settled in St. Catharines, Ontario, Canada. Joe was my mother's brother. When my brother was born, Joe and Anna sent my parents a letter to congratulate them, adding that if our family had another child, he or she would come back with them to Canada. I don't know whether my parents took this seriously, but when my aunt and uncle returned on their six-month visa, it became obvious they were not kidding. Joe and Anna had no children of their own, and Joe, for one, had no use for "those damn Russians." Anyway, one night in the bungalow, they were discussing the subject with my parents. I was hungry, so I broke into the conversation. Mom told me to go back to bed. I started to cry because I wanted a piece of bread, but my mother thought I was crying because my parents didn't want to let me leave. So my mom said, "Okay, take him." Talk about a life-changing moment. What if I hadn't been hungry that night? What if I had just gone to sleep and never cried while my parents resisted saying good-bye to their youngest son?

5

This is a picture of my birth parents, Emilia and George Gvoth, in 1934.

Remember, I was only eight years old and had no idea what was actually happening. I thought I was just taking a little trip, embarking on a nice adventure to another land where Joe and Anna lived like royalty. Living in Czechoslovakia at that time, Canada and United States sounded like heaven. So I jumped on a train to Prague, the first big city I had ever visited. Such tall buildings! No sooner did I look up at one of them than I slammed into a pole. Right in the face. Then we took another train to Le Havre, France, where we got on a boat for a long trip to Canada. A *really* long trip. I want to say it took two or three weeks. I cried (again) when it hit me that going with Joe and Anna meant leaving my parents behind, but the full impact of my adventure really became clear on the ship, *Carinthia*, as we headed toward Montreal. Joe and Anna were on board, of course, but so was a niece, Irene, from Anna's side of the family. She was 11 and although her family, the Gondas, lived near us in Sokolče, I did not know her. While we were on the ship, Irene offered me a stick of gum. She said it was from our father.

"My dad is back in Czechoslovakia," I said. "No," Irene said. "This is from your new dad."

Irene explained that Anna and Joe Mikita, my aunt and uncle, were now our new parents. Irene and I were being adopted. It was halfway through this voyage that I learned what adoption meant. That was the only way we could get out of Czechoslovakia. And now I had a sister, Irene, although two years later, my real parents back in the old country had a daughter of their own, Viera. I later learned that Joe and Anna had only used about 45 days of their six-month visa before leaving with Irene and me. Also, I learned that there had been some conversation about my older brother moving to Canada instead of me. I really don't know how serious that got. Apparently my mother insisted that her first born would stay at home, absolutely and positively. Juraj was easier to handle than I was. That might have influenced her decision to part with me.

7

When we finally arrived in St. Catharines, it was just a few days before Christmas of 1948. My head was spinning. Joe and Anna's house was very nice, a mansion compared with our home in Czecholslovakia. They had electricity instead of kerosene lamps, and they had all these electrical appliances, like an actual refrigerator. Plus, there was a place to cook and a separate place to eat and another place to sleep. And we didn't have to sleep four to a room. All separate, much different from our bungalow in the old country. Another shock to my system occurred when I saw my new mother, Anna, making a lunch for Joe, my new father, to take to work. He was a carpenter. I didn't understand why he had to work because, as I mentioned before, the impression we had in Czechoslovakia was that everybody in Canada and the United States was rich. We didn't think anybody in those lands of milk and honey had to work. Why would you need a job if you had all the money you needed? That was just another part of my education, and it amounted to a crash course in real life. We just figured you went out in the

backyard of your house in Canada and picked dollar bills off the trees.

Was I homesick? From time to time, yes. I couldn't speak a word of English. And every once in a while, I would look up at an airplane in the sky and imagine that it was coming to take me back to Czechoslovakia.

For a while, I even thought I would become a pilot so that I could fly myself back home. (Of course, I don't think I took my first airplane ride until I was around 20.) I was a little ornery at the age of eight, and being in a strange place probably made me even more ornery. I don't know that I was unhappy per se, or even that lonely. Alone, but not necessarily lonely because Joe and Anna were nice to me. I wrote back and forth to my parents quite often, so it wasn't like we didn't stay in touch. My real dad never did come over to Canada or the United States. He died when he was 66. Emilia made a few trips, the first when I got married to my lovely wife, Jill, in 1963.

8

But something was missing for me as a kid trying to figure out my new existence in St. Catharines, and before long, I found something that I loved to fill the void. In the old country, I played mostly soccer except for my one venture onto the pond with my brother's skates. Ice hockey was not on my radar by any means. But as I hung around our house at 57 Hamilton Street, I would peek out the window through the curtains and see a bunch of kids out on the street playing road hockey. One afternoon, right before dinner, I got brave and went outside to see what it was all about. This went on for a couple more days. Each day I got a little closer to the action. Finally, the big guy who seemed to be in charge asked me if I played hockey. His name was Bob Johnson. He was around 15 years old. I somehow got across to him that I didn't speak English, but he took me over to his garage anyway and handed me a stick.

He pointed to me and then to a bunch of kids. That was my team. Then he pointed to the other kids on the other side of the street. That was the other team. I didn't understand every facet of road hockey, but I did know right away that I didn't like kids from the other team

getting around me. It happened once, and I got upset. The next time one of my opponents tried to beat me to the outside, I took my stick and whacked him right across the shins. I was a runt, and this other kid was young, too. Well, he went down like a pile of bricks. Bob came right over to me and I could tell by his gestures and expression that I had done something wrong. Also, the poor kid I hit was on the ground, writhing in pain.

I came back the next day, apologized to the boy I had hurt, and we played again. I learned some new words during those pickup games on Hamilton Street, including a few that I could actually use in mixed company. I also began to learn the skills that would help me later, like how to handle the stick and how to shoot or pass the puck, which was a rubber ball in road hockey. I think I was learning some things about myself too, even at that early juncture in my experience with team sports.

I realized I didn't like to lose or get beaten in one-on-one situations. I was very competitive.

9

Whether I was more competitive than some of the other kids my age, I can't really say. But I do know I cared about how I played. Another lesson came from Joe. He had become quite a good carpenter. He would go into hock, buy a piece of land, build a home on it, and then turn it into a good business proposition. So, after thinking when I came to Canada that nobody had to work because everybody was rich, I learned that the harder you work, the more successful you will be.

\\\\\\\\\\\\\

When I first arrived in St. Catharines, I was put in third grade at Edith Cavell School. I didn't know a word of English, other than that *Stanislav* meant *Stan*. The teachers were great to me, even though I was a challenging student. Maybe they could see that I was lost. I certainly had to look lost—except when it came to numbers. When there was a question about arithmetic, I could figure out the answers in my head. So I would raise my hand. At one point, my teacher, Miss Patterson, suggested that I go back to kindergarten. She talked to Norma Lansky, a girl in the school who was fluent in

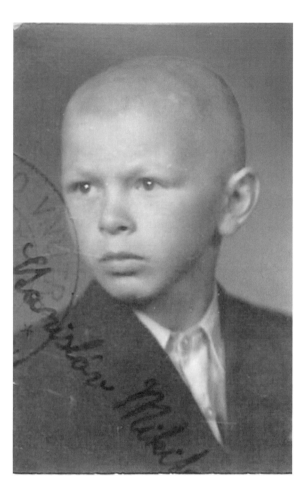

Slovak, her parents, and my parents. Everybody agreed that it would be best if I went back a few grades to work on my English. I was three years older than most of the kids. I was small, but I felt like Goliath. It was a good idea by my teacher. It helped, and after a few weeks, I returned to third grade with a better idea of what to say and what everyone else was saying.

Miss Patterson did me a favor by taking such an interest in me. When I first entered her class, she would speak to me in English. I didn't want to seem more out of place than I already felt, so I would try to fake it and make it seem like I knew what she was saying. She wasn't fooled, though, which is why she recommended that I get "promoted" from third grade to kindergarten. She also told me that I should not be afraid to communicate the best I could when I didn't understand something. Anyone who remembers being in school at that age also remembers the pressure you feel about not wanting to seem different or awkward. My sensitivity was even greater because I was struggling to pick up a new language in a new country. Kids can be cruel. I heard my share of people calling me a "DP", which I eventually realized meant "Displaced Person." It wasn't bad enough that I felt like a foreigner; hearing about it just made it worse. As I got older, I changed the definition of "DP" to "Delayed Pioneer," but I didn't have that going for me in the third grade. Again, my new dad, Joe, taught me about right and wrong when he talked to me about my situation. He said that when he

first got to Canada, he had made the mistake of hanging around people from the old country who spoke Slovak. It was convenient. It was comfortable.

"But don't do what I did," Joe said. "It will be much better for you in the end if you learn English. That will take hard work, but it will be worth it."

Again, that lesson. Hard work. Norma helped me as an interpreter, and I probably viewed learning English as a type of competition, too. My mother tried hard, too. I talked back to her more than I should have, especially when she told me to make my bed every morning after I woke up. But even though I was a hellion on occasion, we became a very close family. In the summer, Joe and Anna sometimes took Irene and me to Toronto for Czechoslovakian Days, which meant picnics and the beach. We did a lot together, including move from house to house. As I said, Joe was good at his job, and every so often, one of those houses he built with his own two hands became our house. My

11

first house in Canada was on Hamilton Street, but it wasn't the last one.

I made friends as I became more accustomed to the surroundings, and one of my best early pals was named Archie Maybe. He came to me one day with a newspaper item. It was about how the Canadian Legion would be starting a hockey league in our area for boys between the ages of 12 and 14. I was still struggling with my English and Archie was struggling with my Slovak, but I managed to communicate two things to him: first, I had never skated in my life, unless you count that brief session I had with my brother's skates back in the old country; and second, what good would it be for either of us to try to sign up for a league of boys between the ages of 12 and 14? This was in the autumn of 1949, so I was only nine and Archie was in my same bracket.

"Let's go anyway," Archie said. "The registration is this Saturday at the Canadian Legion hall."

I was game, so we rode our bikes over that Saturday morning. Archie handled the heavy lifting. When the man behind the desk saw us, he asked if he could be of assistance. Archie

told him we wanted to sign up for hockey. The man asked how old we were. Archie told him the truth: we were not even 10.

"To be honest with you young fellas," the man said, "we're only taking boys who are older than you, as it specified in the newspaper article. Why don't you two come back in a couple years?"

We walked out, and I thought that was that. But Archie was a persistent bugger. He came by the next week, again carrying a newspaper clipping about signups for this new hockey league.

"Let's go and try again this Saturday," he said.

"What good will that do us?" I said in my broken English. "When that man we saw last Saturday behind the desk sees us again, he's just going to throw us out."

"Yeah," said Archie. "But we don't have to go see the same guy. There were two other men taking names behind two other desks. We'll avoid the guy who turned us down and try someone new."

That Archie, I learned a lot from him. Sure enough, we carefully sidestepped the man who

My aunt and uncle, Anna and Joe Mikita, with whom I went to live in 1948 when I was eight years old.

My sister, Irene, my parents, Anna and Joe, and me in St. Catharines, Ontario, in 1950.

had rejected us and went to another desk. A different man asked us the same questions. We lowered our voices slightly and also upped our ages. I told him I was 10½, and Archie said he was almost 11. Lucky for us, we didn't have to show any visual proof, like birth certificates. Lucky for us again, the man said that there hadn't been as many kids signing up as had been expected, so there would be room for us. Bingo!

Now all I had to do was get myself a pair of skates and figure out how to use them. My father Joe was beginning to see how important sports were in my young life, and he was also concerned about the kids I was hanging out with. So, when I asked him after dinner one night about getting a pair of skates, he probably figured it wasn't a bad idea. Nice, wholesome exercise.

Naturally, I was very excited when Joe agreed to get me some skates. Of course, he never said they would be *new* skates. We hopped in the car and drove past a couple sporting goods stores. I kept waiting for Joe to pull in so he could make a purchase. But we didn't stop until he turned the corner and pulled up to a shoe

repair shop. I was puzzled. I didn't need shoes. I needed skates.

"Be quiet," said Joe. "They have what we want here."

Sure enough, they had what Joe wanted. We walked to the back of the store and there were a whole bunch of second-hand skates. The owner of the store asked me what size I needed.

"I'm a size 5," I said.

"Get him a size 8," Joe corrected.

"I can't wear a size 8," I said. "They're too big."

"We'll make them fit," Joe said. "You'll grow into them."

Joe then inquired about whether the store had any socks to sell. They did. He put several pairs in those skates, stuffing them in every which way. Then he told me to try the skates on.

"Perfect," Joe decided. "See? Now they fit you."

So, that's the story about how my father bought me my first pair of skates. I would not recommend this to any parents confronting the same circumstance, because if you provide your son or daughter with skates that are too large,

I was an 11-year-old member of the Edith Cavell School hockey team (first row, third from the left) when this picture was taken in 1951.

"LUCKY FOR US AGAIN,

THE MAN SAID THAT THERE HADN'T

BEEN AS MANY KIDS SIGNING UP AS

HAD BEEN EXPECTED, SO THERE WOULD

BE ROOM FOR US. BINGO!"

—STAN MIKITA

there is a strong chance your child could twist an ankle. Luckily, I never got hurt in those skates, and they actually lasted for three years. I don't know what Joe paid for those skates, but it wasn't much.

\\\\\\\\\\\\

Archie was able to skate and he was aware that I couldn't, so again he came up with a plan. Archie said if we could get to the arena early in the morning, like at 5:00 AM, a friend of his who worked there would let us skate before they opened the rink. Sure enough, we were able to pull this off. I watched everything Archie did and listened to everything he said.

"Take it easy," Archie instructed me. "Keep your balance and take one step at a time."

The chief engineer of the arena in St. Catharines was a man named Vic Teal, who was very well known across Canada and had a couple of sons, Skip and Skeeter, who made it to the NHL. Vic was a good teacher. I retained a lot of what he said. He always carried a broom with him to pick things up around the rink and keep it clean. The broom also served another purpose. If he was trying to get a point across

and you weren't listening, he would raise that broom. Might even give you a little pat on the behind with it for emphasis. Not to hurt you, just to get your attention. He took an interest in me, which I appreciated. He became a mentor of sorts.

> *He would take time out from whatever he was doing, come over to me while I was on the ice, and show me the tricks of the trade.*

I would say he was the first coach who gave me an idea of what it was all about. He saw my spirit, and he said that was a good thing. He also said I had to control myself and my emotions.

I remember checking the newspapers after we signed up to see what team I had been chosen by. I wound up on the Rangers and Archie was on the Canadiens. I took to the skates as best I could and I must have done something right because the two men who were coaching the Rangers, Bill Buschlin and Dennis White, liked what they saw and kept me. I was quite a sight. I had those oversized skates stuffed with socks

and paper, and my shin pads were actually magazines that I had wrapped around my legs for protection. But I tried hard to do well, and eventually hockey became a big part of my life. I played on the Canadian Legion team as well as a team at Edith Cavell. I was on the same team as Archie there because we were both in the same school, at least for a while. Whenever Joe moved us into a different house, I wound up in a different school.

I didn't play much at the start for the Rangers. I was on the bench with the rest of the little guys. Gradually, I played more and more. I never thought of myself as anything special, and the idea of playing hockey as a career or becoming good enough to make the NHL never entered my mind. Besides, it wasn't just hockey that had grabbed my interest. It was all sports. I played lacrosse, for example. And one of the guys I played against was Gerry Cheevers, who went on to become a great goalkeeper with the Boston Bruins. As kids playing lacrosse, we roughed each other up quite a bit, in a respectful way. I also ran into another famous fellow while I was playing football, a boy named Bobby Hull.

Little did either of us know that we would wind up on the Chicago Blackhawks and win a Stanley Cup with them in 1961.

By the time I was 12 years old, I was playing bantam hockey. We won a championship, they threw a banquet for us, and each of us got a wristwatch. You don't think that was a highlight of my life? A real watch with my name on it and everything. Big time. I had new skates by then. Dad had popped for a good pair that cost him $23. I also got some real shin pads and hockey pants. Dad wasn't all that interested in my hockey, nor was Mom. They didn't come to my games for a while, which was fine with me. It might even have been a good thing. Maybe I was more relaxed without them in the building. Along the way, though, Dad got the notion that I was doing more than wasting my time. He would come home at night from work, grab a beer, and pick up the newspaper. Well, my name started popping up in the hockey stories around town. Maybe I had scored a goal or two.

"You do good?" he asked. "We come to see you play."

So Joe and Anna came to a bantam game, and they were sitting in a corner of the rink about halfway up. There were only six or eight rows. I took my first shift, and some kid took a run at me and smashed me into the boards. There was no glass around the rink in those days the way there is now. There was chicken wire, all the better for the noise to travel. And when I fell down into the boards, my stick smashed into the side. That make quite a racket, almost as big a racket as Anna was about to make.

"STANLEY! STANLEY!" she yelled at the top of her lungs. "YOU HURT? GET UP, STANLEY!"

I wasn't hurt, but I was embarrassed. Here I was, in the first game they ever watched me play, and my mother is standing up in the arena, yelling. It got worse. When I got home that night, she said that she didn't want me to play hockey ever again. She thought it was too dangerous. Too rough. No more. I had to beg her to change her mind. After all, I was playing on three different teams. There was the school

team, the Legion team, and then the bantam team, which was the city team. I couldn't quit all of them. I didn't want to leave any of them. Thank goodness she went along with my wishes.

While playing hockey almost all the time, I also attached myself to a couple of groups. One of them was the Facer Street Gang, which was named for the area where we lived. There were Polish kids, Italians, and Slovaks in the gang and they were all mostly older than I was and pretty rough. Fortunately, I wasn't included in all their "activities" because they did some bad things, like steal cars for joyrides every once in a while. I don't remember seeing any guns around them, but I was warned by the local police on more than one occasion to stay away from those guys. Deep down, I didn't feel good about hanging around with them, but it did give me a sense of belonging.

My other group was the Rink Rats, which was comprised of about 10 or 12 kids who took care of the rink where we played. We would do all the dirty jobs, clean the seats, sweep the arena after games, and flood the ice. In exchange for our work, we would get free ice time, usually at 6:00 in the morning when Vic Teal showed up.

21

Some of us were already there because there were a few cots in the Rink Rats room, so we would sometimes spend the night there. After school, we would return to the rink to skate some more, then maybe play a pickup game after the public left. My parents didn't seem to mind me spending all those hours at the rink. First, I was doing well enough in school, so they didn't have to worry about my grades. Second, they knew I was hooked on hockey. Finally, Vic Teal was such a respected man in the community, they knew I was in good hands. He didn't just teach me a lot about life; he constantly drilled me, and the other kids, on the mechanics of the game. I was at the stage where I had some idea of the basics, but still was way short on a lot of fundamentals. I didn't really know how to body check. I didn't know how to skate clockwise. Most kids lead with the right foot crossing over. He would make us practice leading with the right. He also taught me how to keep a guy between the boards and my body without doing something illegal or stupid, like using my fists.

Despite the guidance and time Teal devoted to us, I can't say the Rink Rats were involved in only humanitarian pursuits. We weren't all Rhodes Scholars, to be sure. I was smoking cigarettes by the time I was 12. My parents didn't know, at least at the start. Eventually, they must have found a few of them jammed in my pockets. They questioned me and I confessed. I said I was sorry, although I don't ever remember saying I would quit. I also had my first taste of beer, but I didn't like it. Duty compels me to report that my attitude changed over the years. I even had a brief spat with Teal at one point. I was around him for several years, trying to be a good soldier, but once I got into it with him and swore. He told me to leave the rink and never come back. Two days later, I returned to apologize. He didn't buy it. Then I started crying and he decided to give me another chance.

Vic had a big heart, and later on in life he admitted that he saw something in me that he really liked. "You always wanted to be the best," he said.

\\\\\\\\\\\\\

I didn't have any visions of playing in the NHL as a kid because I never saw the NHL, in person or on television. We didn't have a TV set. Maybe that's why I wasn't all that impressed when I was 12 and attending Victoria School, where the principal was Ashton Morrison. At one time Morrison had been president of the Ontario Minor Hockey Association and had become friends with Frank Selke Jr., general manager of the mighty Montreal Canadiens. Because of their association, a few Canadiens came to our school one day. The Canadiens were playing the Toronto Maple Leafs in an exhibition game in St. Catharines, so Morrison had some stars drop by. Maurice "Rocket" Richard, Boom Boom Geoffrion, and Doug Harvey were among them. That's pretty fancy company, not that I knew it at the time. I had no hockey heroes or idols, and the only reason I asked for autographs was because it seemed like the thing to do. Other kids were asking, so I followed along.

Morrison was fond of me. We won the city public school championship at Victoria in 1953. Then, in 1954, we moved to another of

My mother, Emilia Gvoth

Dad's new houses, and I enrolled at the Prince of Wales School. What do you know? Mr. Morrison had moved there too, and we won another championship that year. The coach at Prince of Wales was Jim Patterson, who was also helpful to my progress. He tried to stress sportsmanship to me, clean play and all that good stuff. Notice I say, he *tried*. I was not a good loser. But I did play hard, and Morrison took note. During that visit by the Canadiens to Victoria School, Selke jokingly pointed to his legends—Richard, Geoffrion, and Harvey—and asked Morrison if he would like to make a deal for one of those future Hall of Famers. Morrison answered, "No, I wouldn't trade Mikita for any of them." I suspect he was just trying to make me feel good about myself.

Despite my size, or lack thereof, I liked to hit people.

I don't know where my aggression stemmed from, but it might have had something to do with feeling like an outsider for so long. My enjoyment of contact helped me in football, where I played safety. I was small for a catcher, but that's the position I played in baseball because I could really throw the ball (at least until I broke my shoulder playing hockey). I had heard in my later teens that the Philadelphia Phillies and Chicago White Sox were actually looking at me as a possible prospect. After I hurt my shoulder, though, I couldn't even throw the ball across a room. Wouldn't that have been something? If

I wound up as an athlete in Chicago, but with the White Sox instead of the Blackhawks?

As it turned out, the Blackhawks had an eye on me from the time I was a bantam, which encompassed players who were 12 or 13 (midget was for kids 14 and 15). The Blackhawks, who had been down and out for a long while, had developed a sponsorship with the St. Catharines Teepees, a junior team. The Blackhawks thereby had the territorial rights to me even before I knew what the heck territorial rights meant. Things were much different then. Now, there is a universal draft. The Canadiens, for instance, had territorial rights to all the best players in Quebec, which was quite an advantage and probably one reason why the rules changed on who belonged to whom. A universal, or common, draft is the accepted system in all other sports. If you play college basketball in Utah, that doesn't mean you have to play for the professional team in Utah if you're good enough to make the National Basketball Association.

Anyway, Rudy Pilous was the coach with the Teepees, and he seemed to be aware of absolutely everything that was going on in town. He hung around the rink quite a bit, so I got to

24

know him. By the time I was 16 and done with midget hockey, I was at a fork in the road. Was I going to screw around with the guys in town, or was I going to take hockey seriously? To that end, I wondered whether I could possibly get a tryout with the Teepees. Rudy didn't mince any words. He told me to clean up my act. Get a haircut, wash behind my ears, and look the part of a player instead of a punk. If I did those things, I would get my tryout.

As I look back on the amazing series of events and consequences that shaped my life, I scratch my head and give thanks.

If you had written a script and tried to sell my story to a director for a movie, he'd have laughed at you. Not believable enough. Kid leaves Czechoslovakia at the age of eight, can't speak a word of English, winds up living with loving new parents in a hockey hotbed like St.

Catharines, is just dumb enough to hang out with a bad crowd but just smart enough to realize that he had to break away, and becomes good enough to earn a living by playing a game he loves. Crazy. If I hadn't left Czechoslovakia, I probably would have joined the army or maybe the Communist party or, with my attitude, been sent to Siberia.

My mother, Emilia, came to the United States several times and saw the lifestyle I enjoyed in Chicago with my wife, Jill, and our wonderful children. Shortly before she died in 1996, Jill and I were visiting her in her home. I recall one instance when Mom became quiet and very pensive. She was quiet, thinking, pondering. Then she just looked up at me and, out of nowhere, said, "I made the right decision."

As I look back on the amazing series of events and consequences that shaped my life, I scratch my head and give thanks.

BOBBY HULL

The first time I saw Stan Mikita on the ice, I was practicing with my junior team, the St. Catharines Teepees. I looked across the rink and there was this kid with this haircut, short in the middle and combed back on the side. I asked who that kid was and was told he was a youngster who hadn't been in town long. He's from the old country, I was told, and he can really play. If ever a scouting report was right on the money, that was it.

We wound up in school together, playing other sports together, and eventually we wound up on the same line with the Teepees, when Stan came aboard a year after me. We weren't together too long, mind you. It didn't take long for Rudy Pilous, our coach, to figure out that I was too dumb to be a center and Stan was too smart to be a right winger. So I switched to left wing and Stan moved to center. That's where we played for the rest of our lives, and I was privileged to be with Stan in Chicago, where he became, I believe, the greatest pound-for-pound hockey player who ever played. I don't have to tell you how skilled he was with the puck, and despite his size he was tougher than a night in jail.

Stan was a little chippy, trying to protect himself from guys who ran at him. Stan didn't have the kind of protection a lot of guys his size had as far as teammates looking after him. As a result, Stan took a lot of penalties in the early years. But he gradually evolved into a great scorer and a Lady Byng winner. When Stan first came up, he stayed with Tod Sloan, Ron Murphy, and me out in the western suburb of Berwyn. Four beds in two rooms, and a 1949 Chevy with a hole in the floor to get us around. What a machine that was.

We socialized a bit in juniors. Stan would get the truck from his dad on occasion and we'd double date, Stan and his girl in the front, me and mine on potato crates in the back. We always got along, Stan and me. For some reason, there were these stories by people, I don't know who they were, about how we were rivals and how we weren't friendly and all that. Nothing could be further from the truth. We were different personalities and different types of players, but we always got along and always had the same objective in mind—to win hockey games.

I just wish we could have played together on the same line, which we rarely did. You look around the National Hockey League during our time in Chicago. It was common for a team's best scorers to be on the same line together. But for some reason, it just never happened with the Blackhawks. Granted, he was a playmaker who wanted the puck and I was a scorer who wanted the puck. But can you imagine the damage we would have done together? I don't know the exact thinking behind keeping us separate. Maybe to spread us out. Maybe the theory was that it made it more difficult for the opposition if Stan and I weren't out there together. I can't say for sure. Stan and I both had pretty good careers and we both put up some pretty good numbers. But if we had been together for any length of time, it would have been scary. Stan could find you in the dark. He could thread a needle with his passing. He made everything look so easy. He was so bloody smart. I tell you, if he and I could have been on the same line, it would have been something.

Bobby Hull scored 604 goals, the most in Blackhawks history, from 1957 to 1972. He was inducted into the Hockey Hall of Fame in 1983, the same year his No. 9 was retired by the Blackhawks. He is currently a team ambassador.

STAN MIKITA
1ST NHL GOAL
NEW YORK AT CHICAGO
OCTOBER 7, 1959

"To be making $25 a week to play hockey seemed like all the money in the world."

—STAN MIKITA

CHAPTER TWO

THE ROAD TO THE NHL

When I was 16, it was time for Junior-A hockey and the St. Catharines Teepees. That meant a possible stepping stone to something bigger and better. The Junior-A system was the top of the line for players who were still amateurs, and above that was the minor league system, in which you were a professional. There really wasn't much high school hockey in Canada, and in those days, it was unusual for Canadian kids to attend college and then play in the NHL. Obviously, it's a lot different now. Junior-A was a developmental league where kids like me played. The minors had kids too, but they also had some older players who were waiting their turn in the NHL or had maybe been sent down because they needed more seasoning or because the rosters of their NHL teams were full. Don't forget, there were only six NHL franchises back then, and the teams' rosters were smaller. NHL teams carried only 16 players and one goalie. If a goalie got hurt during a game, there was an emergency goalie in each building who could be called upon to play for *either* team. That sounds unbelievable now in an era when all 30 NHL teams are required to dress two goalies for every game, but that's the way it was back then.

If you were considered a pretty good prospect, you played Junior-A hockey. A step below that was Junior-B, and then there was the Juvenile League for kids ages 16 to 18. If you were over 18 and didn't graduate to at least Junior-B, you really didn't have a place to play. So, I guess by getting a tryout with the Junior-A Teepees, I was considered a decent prospect. I was probably 5'6" and maybe 140 pounds. I would like to say I was growing like a weed, but I wasn't. When I turned pro at age 18, I was 5'8" and 152 pounds.

Anyway, the difference between midget hockey and playing with the Teepees was huge. I was an adolescent, and so were most of the other guys. But the big adjustment was the speed of everything. It seemed like everything in Junior-A was twice as fast as anything I had experienced before. As I mentioned, Rudy Pilous' office was in the rink where I played when I was younger, and you never knew when he was there or when he was looking out on the ice. I knew that Rudy was a head honcho of some sort. Eventually, I learned that he was in charge of the Teepees, who had won a Memorial Cup in 1954, which was a big deal in Canada.

That's the championship of Junior-A hockey. The Teepees beat the Edmonton Oil Kings in five games under Rudy, so he had become a legend. The Teepees won another Memorial Cup in 1960, after I was gone.

Along the way, I also learned that you could actually get paid for playing hockey. The idea that you could make money for doing something you enjoyed shocked me, to be honest.

But you've got to understand my background. Almost all the kids my age grew up in Canada, where hockey was like a religious experience. When you were four or five years old, you started to skate and watch NHL games and dreamed about becoming a hockey player. When I was four or five, I was still back in the old country. A lot of the kids in junior hockey also had to leave home at an early age to play with their designated team. Bobby Hull, for instance, was born in Point Anne, Ontario, not terribly far from St. Catharines but far enough that he had to pack up and live with another family so he could play with the Teepees. His mom and dad traveled to watch him play. Meanwhile, by living in St. Catharines, I was able to sleep in my own bed. I had traveled a long way to get there from Czechoslovakia, so as far as leaving home early, I guess I had a head start on some of the other guys.

My tryout went well, and Rudy indicated that I could make the team. It was then that the reality of being paid hit me between the eyes. I had to sign a contract. Rudy brought me into his office and told me he liked the way things were going. He then said that he would pay me $25 a week to start the season with the Teepees. If I played well enough to stay with the team beyond Christmas of 1956, I would get a raise to $35 a week. When I heard that, I had an instant reaction. Are you kidding me? Where do I sign? I don't know how much money I had saved to that point, but it wasn't much, that's for sure. To be making $25 a week to play hockey seemed like all the money in the world. I accepted Rudy's proposal on the spot. I was thrilled to be getting paid to play hockey, and I was even more thrilled when I started seeing those paychecks roll in.

I was still in school then at St. Catharines Collegiate Institute, and even though the Teepees tried to arrange practices around classes, my interest in studying started to fade a bit. My parents were on board with me playing hockey as long as I did my homework. Whenever we went on a road trip, I brought books with me on the bus. I'm not sure how often I opened them, to be honest, but it wasn't like we were going across the country. Road games were always within 100 miles, at the most.

Bobby Hull and I first met in school. We played football together, although not exactly the same way.

He was big when he was little, if you know what I mean, so when Bobby took the ball as a halfback, he basically ran over and through people. I tried to run around the opponents or at least follow my blocking. Bobby and I were only teammates for one year on the Teepees, and he played hockey a lot like he played football. He just skated over guys or through them or both.

In 1956–57, his second year with the Teepees, Bobby scored 33 goals in 52 games. I couldn't believe that he had such an impressive build but was just a year or so older than me. I found out that he didn't lift weights, either. During the summers he would lift 80-pound bags of cement onto trucks when he wasn't lifting those bales of hay on the farm. He didn't need to go to the gym, not that any of us worked out like the modern players do now. That was my first year, 1956–57, and I had 16 goals and 31 assists in 52 games. We played together on a line, but only for a very short time. I guess Rudy figured out that we'd need two pucks with both of us out there together, which might not have been far from the truth. Bobby had started out as a center, but Rudy switched him to left wing. I played right wing with him, but that changed, too. Before long, Rudy moved me from right wing to center. When I look back at some of the pivotal moments in my career, that certainly had to be one—the day I came to practice and saw that Rudy had me on the chart as a center.

"What's going on here?" I asked. "I don't know how to be a center. I've never been one. I have no idea what to do."

Pilous was always thinking. And thinking ahead.

"It's just an experiment," he said. "Look at the team in Chicago. They have some centers, but they're getting on in age. Like Tod Sloan, like Glen Skov. Plus, they're pretty well-situated at right wing. I believe if you want to make the Blackhawks, your best shot is as a center. Also, centers make a little more money than right wings, you know. I think you can do it. You handle the puck well, on the forehand and backhand, you can pass the puck either way, you certainly can skate, and you can stick-handle the puck. I'd like you to try it and see what happens."

I was just a kid, and Rudy Pilous was a giant in the business. Who was I to argue with him? I thought he was crazy, but naturally I never said as much. I thought that I had a fairly good grasp on the fundamentals, but to change positions all of a sudden seemed like a pretty dramatic development.

"Does this mean I can only skate up and down the middle of the ice?" I asked.

"No, no, you can go all over," Pilous said. "You'll learn. Don't forget, I've been watching

since you were a bantam. I think I have a pretty good idea of what you can and can't do."

Evidently, I didn't screw it up too badly, because center is where I played the rest of my life.

The responsibilities were different than being a winger, offensively and defensively, but one thing I always felt I was pretty good at was passing the puck. Naturally, that's a major part of being a center. You still have to shoot the puck, but your real job is to be a playmaker. I've got to thank Pilous in retrospect for taking that gamble on me. It was a challenge for me, which was fine, and Rudy had a great ability to sell you on something. He had the gift of gab. He had a million stories and he would fire up the kids in Junior-A with his pregame speeches. He was a good teacher who could see flaws and try to correct them without beating you over the head with advice. Most of his criticisms took place in private, and if you played a good game, he was quick to tell you so. Rudy also made a point to both Bobby and me that if we wanted

to play hockey for him, we weren't going to be playing any more football in school.

At the start of my second season with the Teepees, I went in for another contract negotiation with Pilous. My price was $50 a week, up from $35.

"I had a pretty good first season," I said. "I think I deserve a raise."

"I agree," Pilous said, "but I don't think we can afford to pay you what you want, Stan. I'll pay you $40 a week."

I wasn't such an easy mark anymore. I told Pilous that I would not come down from $50 a week, even if he proposed splitting the difference and paying me $45 a week. If I didn't get what I wanted, I wasn't going to play. How about that! Pilous huffed and puffed and finally agreed to pay me $50 a week, which was still below the limit. In those days, the top salary for a Junior-A player was $60 a week, even though I heard all sorts of rumors about how some players were being paid a little more under the table, not to mention the stories about how junior teams also threw in a few bucks for some players' families. Eventually, I put the pinch on the Teepees for $15 a week to give to my mother for room and board. After all, I was living at home. Why shouldn't I get some money for that? I wound up getting it in cash, so it didn't show up on the books as part of my salary. I was happy and my mother was thrilled. I have no idea what my father was making at the time, but I sure liked those checks rolling in every two weeks.

In the middle of the 1957–58 season, Pilous got the call from Chicago to coach the Blackhawks. Tommy Ivan had been doing two jobs, general manager and coach, and it became too much. So Rudy went to the NHL, and Glen Sonmor finished out that season as coach of the Teepees. Sonmor, a good guy, played a little bit in the NHL before an injury cost him his vision in one eye. He went on to coach the Minnesota North Stars after the NHL expanded from six to 12 teams. I had a good second year, scoring 31 goals and assisting on 47 others. The next year, our coach was Harry Watson, another former NHL player, and we had a heck of a team. Pat Stapleton, Matt Ravlich, and Wayne Hillman were on defense, Denis DeJordy was our goalie, and at forward we had John McKenzie, Chico

Maki, and Vic Hadfield. All of them would make it to the NHL. It was during that season that I began contemplating turning pro and making hockey my occupation.

One event that triggered by imagination occurred in November of 1958. I was having dinner at home when the phone rang. Watson was on the other end. Pack your bags, he told me. You're going to Chicago. You're going to play tomorrow night.

"Harry," I said. "You're playing with me. That can't be."

"No, it's true," he said. "You've got to catch a midnight train out of Welland for Chicago. I'll pick you up at your house about 10:00 and drive you to the station."

I still didn't believe him, and I didn't begin gathering my belongings until he showed up. He explained that Sloan had gotten hurt in Chicago, and my old coach, Rudy Pilous, had asked for me. I was still an amateur, of course, and there weren't many amateurs who made the jump from juniors to the NHL without stopping in the minors—not that I was guaranteed anything when I got to Chicago. I must have been cordial or even friendly with

"ONCE IN A WHILE, MY FATHER WOULD LET ME BORROW THE TRUCK FOR A NIGHT, AND WE WOULD DOUBLE DATE—BOBBY AND HIS GIRL, ME AND MINE—AT THE DRIVE-IN MOVIE."

—STAN MIKITA

the press guys in those days because they had been writing some articles in the Canadian papers about how I was the "best junior player in Canada." I didn't pay much attention to the stories, or at least I tried not to, but my dad was reading them.

Anyway, Watson took me to the train station in Welland, where I was expecting to have a place to sleep on the overnight trip to Chicago. When I showed my ticket to the conductor, I found out differently.

I was in an old wooden chair, not a sleeper car. I didn't get a wink of sleep, and because of those fancy accommodations, my back was killing me the next morning when I arrived in Chicago at the LaSalle Street station. Naturally, I had no idea where I was or where I was supposed to go, so I went to a nearby coffee shop and lit up a cigarette. I was excited, probably a little nervous, and definitely tired. I also thought Bobby was going to be the one

who would meet me. But the next voice I heard was Rudy's.

"What are you doing smoking?" he growled. "Put that thing out."

Pilous knew that I had smoked, but he thought I quit. Which I had, until I quit quitting. When I was really smoking up a storm, I was good for a pack a day. Rudy took me to the Chicago Stadium, where I met the trainer, Nick Garen, who fixed me up with all the equipment I needed. Pilous then suggested that since I would be in Chicago for at least a couple days, I should stay with Bobby, who was sharing an apartment in the western suburbs with Sloan and Ron Murphy. So, I got on a bus and went west until I met Bobby at the end of the line.

"Welcome to Chicago," he said. Here we were, a couple of kids from the Teepees, now in the NHL with the Blackhawks.

The big difference is that he was already in the process of establishing himself as a star, but he was nice to me as always, and it was nice to see him. We had known each other for a while. Back in St. Catharines, when we weren't playing football or hockey, we would socialize a bit. Once in a while, my father would let me borrow the truck for a night, and we would double date—Bobby and his girl, me and mine—at the drive-in movie. In juniors, Bobby could fire the puck like nobody else, but he didn't always hit the net with it. He was a little wild, and I used to joke with him about it. Obviously, as he matured, Bobby was able to find the net quite often, thank you very much.

"I know you're up here as an emergency replacement," Bobby told me. "But I'm sure you'll be up here in Chicago for good before too long. Just do what you do in St. Catharines. You'll be fine."

Pilous gave me much the same advice for my NHL debut, which came against the Montreal Canadiens at the Chicago Stadium. I had seen only one NHL game in my entire life. One time the Teepees had an afternoon game in Toronto and we got standing-room-only tickets to watch the Maple Leafs that night in Maple Leaf Gardens. So the second game I ever saw was one in which I played, and who did I wind up taking my first faceoff against but Jean Beliveau? Rudy did me a favor by putting me on a line between Ed Litzenberger and Ted Lindsay, who became a mentor of sorts for me. But I was still in a daze when I went out to take that faceoff against a legend like Beliveau, who was around 6'5" and a towering presence on the ice. He had to outweigh me by 60 pounds. The faceoff was in Montreal's end. I looked up at him from the circle and I wound up staring at his belly button. That's how tall he was. My knees were shaking. My head was spinning. Somehow I got my stick down and managed to get the puck back to our point man. Don't ask me who it was. I was too nervous to remember names. But I do recall that we got a shot off on Jacques Plante, another legend who was in goal for the Canadiens.

Later on the same shift, I wound up with the puck against defenseman Doug Harvey, yet another future Hall of Famer. I decided to give him a fake to the right, it worked, and I got the puck through his legs and on Plante, who made a kick save. I was pretty proud of my debut, at least until Tom Johnson, Harvey's defensive partner, caught me with my head down and checked me from here to there. I felt it, but I didn't want to let on that I was hurt or anything. I didn't wind up on the score sheet in my first game, but I did play three games total for the Blackhawks that season, and I did register one assist on a goal by Lindsay. As I recall, I made $100 per game as an amateur. You were allowed to play five games in those days as an amateur without being required to turn professional.

Besides those brief pit stops with the Blackhawks, my 1958–59 season was spent in St. Catharines, where I continued to enjoy playing while I pondered my future. I really had no career plans, per se. Like a lot of kids, I did odd jobs when I wasn't playing games. Vic Teal had set me up with a job at the beach one summer. I was asked whether I wanted to be a lifeguard—no doubt because of my strapping physique—but I passed on it. I didn't think it would be a good idea since I didn't know how to swim. Later, Pilous fixed me up at the local racetrack in Fort Erie, where I was a pari-

mutuel clerk. I didn't know anything about horses, although I started picking up tips from guys around there who dropped hints. I made a few bets and won a few dollars and started thinking it was a pretty nice hobby. Of course, sooner or later you get tips that don't pan out and you wind up giving back a lot of the money you won, or all of it, or more.

I can't deny that the concept of becoming a pro hockey player interested me. My father was doing well enough to have saved money for me to go to college, so there was no pressure on me financially. In fact, my parents probably wanted me to finish high school, which I had pretty much abandoned, then get a college education. A couple of colleges did offer me athletic scholarships. Meanwhile, I reasoned that I could always turn pro, try to make the NHL, play three or four years if I could, save some money, and then go do something else. Don't ask me what that something else was. I stopped going to classes when I was 18, which was Grade 11, after which my dad said, "Why do you think I work so hard? So I can put you through school. That's what I promised

your parents back in Czechoslovakia when we brought you to Canada. You could be a lawyer. You got brains. You are smart." But the more I got into hockey, the more school seemed like a chore.

> ### *I could have been going to class when I wasn't on the ice playing hockey, but I wound up going to the movies with my teammates instead.*

Of course, the more I played hockey and the better I got, the more interested my father became. The man who never went to my games when I was 12 gladly used the tickets to games when I was 18. He became an instant expert, God bless him. He'd say, "What's the matter with you, son? Why did you pass the puck last night when you had an open net?" Despite the press clippings, I really had no idea whether I was good enough to make it to the NHL. I was confident and probably a bit cocky, but I did not automatically see myself in Chicago with the Blackhawks, at least not right away. I figured

that if I turned pro, I would probably wind up with their farm team in Buffalo. Those cameo appearances with the Blackhawks certainly didn't hurt my confidence, but it was still a giant leap to go from Junior-A to the NHL without making that stop in the minors. I did manage to win the league scoring title in 1958–59 with the Teepees. I had 38 goals and 59 assists for 97 points in only 45 games because of an injury. At the Junior-A all-star game, I broke my wrist. I kept playing, but about a month later I dislocated my right shoulder after sliding into the boards. I heard something snap, then when I went to the bench, I realized I couldn't lift my arm. I had surgery, and that was the end of my season. Also, it was the end of my time with the St. Catharines Teepees.

I wish I could say that was the scariest injury I suffered as a kid, but it wasn't. When I was a midget, we were in a playoff game and Carl Brewer, who later became a star defenseman with the Maple Leafs, flipped the puck out of his end on his backhand. He had a habit of doing that, but I was skating right toward him and the blade of his stick gouged my nose

I appreciated Lindsay's advice, but I think he was
working on salary figures from a few years back.

and cheek. I was bleeding like a stuck pig up through the eyelid and eyebrow, right up to my forehead. I was rushed to the hospital and took around 30 stitches, then went home and went straight to bed. I had a terrible headache. My parents were out for the night, but when they returned, Mom came to my room, turned on the light, and saw me with this huge, bloody bandage over my face. She thought I had lost an eye. In truth, I was lucky that I hadn't. Brewer's stick missed my eye by less than an inch.

My mother was horrified, and she screamed, "That's it, no more hockey for you! You are going to kill yourself." It wasn't the first time I'd heard that.

\\\\\\\\\\\\

By the time I finally made the move to turn pro in the summer of 1959, I realized that some of

the guys I had played against were advancing to the minor leagues or the NHL even though they didn't match the numbers that I had produced in St. Catharines. I didn't think I was the greatest thing since sliced bread, but when I received a letter inviting me to the Blackhawks' training camp, I wanted to make sure I got a fair contract. Nobody ever taught me how to negotiate a deal, but somewhere along the line I must have decided I didn't want to be taken advantage of. I talked to a few of the veterans on the team, notably Ted Lindsay, who had been traded to Chicago from Detroit after he explored the idea of starting up a players' union. The idea didn't fly with Jack Adams, who ran the Red Wings, so Lindsay got traded. When I asked Ted about what I should ask for upon turning pro, he said that I should not settle for anything less than $7,000 a year. Mind you, in those days what guys made was a complete secret. You didn't ask about another player's salary, and you weren't told. Now, you can see entire team payrolls in the newspaper.

I appreciated Lindsay's advice, but I think he was working on salary figures from a few years back. At the time I was ready to turn pro, the NHL minimum had already "exploded" to $7,500 a year. For some reason, I settled on wanting $8,500 a year and a two-year commitment. Naturally, I had to get that past Tommy Ivan, the Blackhawks general manager who was quickly earning his reputation as one of the toughest negotiators around. His initial offer was the minimum, $7,500 a year, or $4,000 a year on a minor league contract if I didn't make the Blackhawks and had to be sent to their Buffalo farm team.

"Mr. Ivan," I said, "that will not be enough."

"Well," he said, "how much do you want?"

"I want two years at $9,000 a year," I said.

"My boy," said Ivan, "we can't pay you that. Where do you think we're going to get that kind of money? We can't pay that to an untried rookie."

Ivan was a very dapper dresser and very serious when it came to talking money. He often managed to throw in a "my boy" just for emphasis. I had no leverage, of course, because

none of us players did. But I didn't feel out of place during my brief NHL fling, and although I wasn't completely hooked on making a career out of hockey, I felt I could make a go of it.

"Mr. Ivan," I said. "That's what I think I'm worth and I'm not going to sign for less."

"What makes you so sure that you'll make the big club?" he asked.

"I believe I will," I said. Then he changed the subject to the other half of the discussion.

"Well," he said, "what about the minor league contract?"

I told him $4,000 a year wasn't enough, either. At this point, he became a little irritated and told me again that the maximum he would pay for an NHL contract was $7,500. Then he asked me to think it over for a while. Which I did, for about a week, until I heard from him again. He asked me whether I had changed my mind. I told him no. Then he upped the offer to $8,000. Again, I said no. Without an agreement, I continued to practice and play with the Blackhawks right until the last day of training camp. I knew I could fall back on the fact that I had a year of eligibility left as an amateur, but I didn't want to go that route.

I wasn't really worried, especially since I had been doing pretty well on the ice. The way I sized things up, I looked to be the fourth center on the roster.

"Our final offer," he said, "is for $8,000, and that's completely fair."

"I'll settle for $8,500 a year and two years," I said.

"Well, okay, you've got it," he said. "Now, what about the minor league contract?"

I told him again that I didn't plan on playing in the minor leagues and he said he hoped I was right. But we still had to put something on paper. Eventually, we agreed to $5,500 a year if I was sent to Buffalo. Then I brought up the subject of a signing bonus. I had heard through my conversations with the guys that it was common for a player to receive a little extra upon completing a deal. He was ready and offered $2,000.

"I want $5,000," I said. He laughed for a minute, then agreed. We shook hands and I left the office feeling pretty good about things. I wound up getting exactly what I wanted. In a way, I used Lindsay's advice about how to survive in the NHL. He wasn't a big guy either, and when I asked him one day how he had lasted in the league for so long—he began his career with the Red Wings in 1944 and wasn't more than 160 pounds—Lindsay said, "Kid, hit 'em first." In other words, be aggressive and don't back down because of your size and your youth. I suppose I applied some of the same thought processes in my talks with Ivan.

Lindsay's words of wisdom were certainly valuable during the games themselves. I had been tested in junior hockey and I didn't expect it to be any different in the NHL, where the talent level

If you didn't like what some guy did to you during a Saturday night road game, you didn't have to wait long to return the favor.

44

was higher and the style of play was much faster and a lot more physical. I was a young punk, and it didn't take me long to figure out which guys on the other teams were going to try me. There were plenty of them, believe me. And in those days, you could get away with a lot more than you can now. The rules today don't allow for as much slashing, hooking, or interference as you saw in the six-team NHL.

That was also another big difference. With only five other opponents over a 70-game regular season schedule, we played each team 14 times. Often, there were home-and-home series on the weekends. We might play in Montreal on a Saturday night, then jump on a train—both teams in separate cars—to Chicago, where we would have a return match on Sunday night. That type of familiarity built up very intense rivalries and grudges. If you didn't like what some guy did to you during a Saturday night road game, you didn't have to wait long to return the favor. In the current NHL, with two conferences of 15 teams each, you might not see another team for a month. As an example, the Boston Bruins and Blackhawks

had some real battles back in the day. But in 2010, the two teams played only one game in Boston in late March. The Bruins never even came to Chicago.

I always said I would go back to finish school, one way or another, but that never happened. Once I got going in the NHL, that was my focus in the winters, and the summers were for resting and healing up. Hockey in Chicago was still coming out of a dark period in the team's history. The Blackhawks made the playoffs in 1953 for the first time since 1946. During that period, attendance had dropped so low that there were actually rumors about the team not being able to survive in Chicago and having to move, maybe to St. Louis. In 1958–59, the year I played just three games as an amateur, the Blackhawks made the playoffs but were eliminated in the first round.

Glenn Hall, our goalie, joked about how bad the crowds were when he first came over from Detroit in the Lindsay trade. He said you could hear what the people were saying in the stands and that if a guy brought his wife, that would double the number of fans in one

45

section. He also said that if a kid walked down Michigan Avenue with a hockey stick in his hands, he might be arrested because nobody knew what it was. When I started my first full year with the Blackhawks in 1959–60, it wasn't that bad. I could see some people in the old Stadium, and one of my first impressions was how excited they became when Bobby skated out for his shift. They were waiting for him to unleash that slap shot of his.

There were a fair number of tough guys in the league, yes, but there were also some smaller players that were more my size. The Rangers had a very good forward, Camille Henry, who was skinnier than I was. I always promised myself that size would not hold me back, nor would effort. I would not fail for lack of trying. When I was about to start the 1959–60 season, Rudy Pilous told me to just go out there and play my game. Don't rely on one move, he said, because other teams will catch on to what you are doing. He told me to keep varying my style and to keep trying different things. Finally, he told me to never stop learning. Just because I was in the NHL didn't mean I would make it big in the NHL.

On October 7, 1959, we opened the regular season against the New York Rangers at the Stadium. I was the center between Bobby Hull and Eric Nesterenko. During one of our shifts, Bobby fired the puck, it hit me in the behind, and went into the net behind New York's goalie, Gump Worsley.

It was my first NHL goal. It wasn't a work of art, but I didn't care.

I dove into the net to grab the puck so I could keep it as a souvenir. I had only seven more the rest of the season, but I stayed with the Blackhawks and never did have to play one game in the minor leagues. Joe and Anna always wanted me to make something of myself. They promised my parents back in Czechoslovakia that they would raise me and educate me in Canada and help me become a success.

Well, I had done it. I had become a professional hockey player with the Chicago Blackhawks.

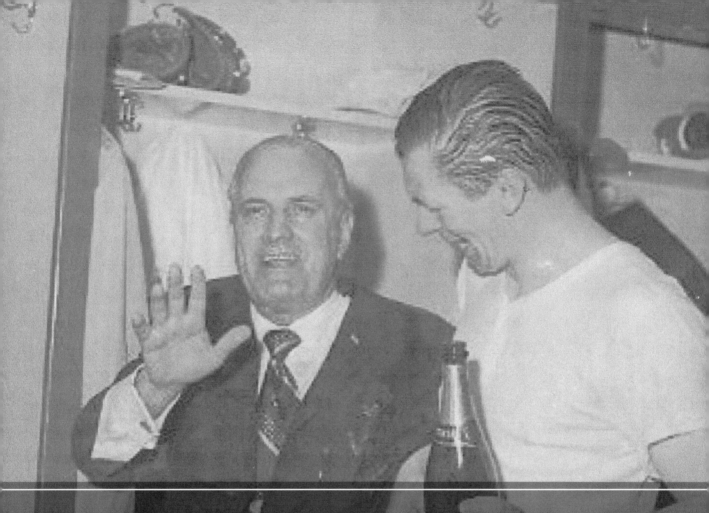

"Hockey had become huge in Chicago after a long, dark period, and with the team we had, I thought we would win it all over and over again. I thought we had the secret. I thought we were a dynasty."

—STAN MIKITA

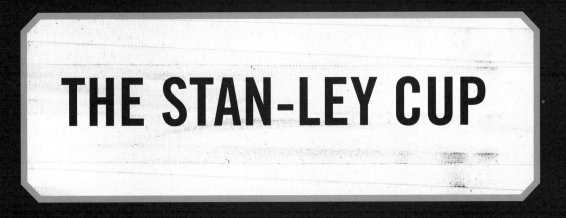

CHAPTER THREE

THE STAN-LEY CUP

I f I had to give myself a grade for my first full year with the Blackhawks, I would give myself an F. I had only eight goals and 18 assists in 67 games in 1959–60, along with 119 penalty minutes. Whenever I saw Tommy Ivan hanging around, I thought he was about to tap me on the shoulder and tell me I was being sent to the minors. It was one thing to make it to the NHL, but another thing to *stay* in the NHL. Fortunately, I never got sent to Buffalo, but that didn't mean I didn't think about it.

We had a few extra guys at training camp before that season, and I knew they weren't going to keep more bodies than they had to because that meant they would have to be paid. One of the players in camp was Phil Maloney, who was a center, just like me. In the first 10 exhibition games—we played a lot more exhibition games and had a longer training camp in those days than they do now—Maloney scored 10 goals and I had only three. On those numbers alone, Maloney could have gotten the nod, but he was a lot older than I was. Rudy Pilous reminded me of that during one of our conversations. "You have your age going for you," he said. "If you sign your contract, looks like we might be stuck with you."

When camp broke in St. Catharines, a few of our guys went to the annual All-Star Game. Back then, the All-Star Game was played at the start of the regular season and featured the previous year's Stanley Cup champions against the stars from the rest of the teams. The Canadiens had just won again, so Glenn Hall went to Montreal and asked me to drive his Ford station wagon back to Chicago. It was full of stuff and I was glad to do it. He had children so there were lots of clothes on board. That was another of my introductions to the world of professional hockey, driving a teammate's vehicle from Canada to the United States. I made the club and I scored my first goal early, but there weren't too many afterward. And, as you can tell by my 119 penalty minutes, I had my share of disagreements with opposing players, a few of whom had tried to run over me.

I didn't take kindly to that kind of treatment, so I probably deserved most of those penalties. I think Hall was the guy who took me aside early in that season and suggested that I didn't have to get back at guys five minutes after they had beaten the crap out of me. We play a lot of games against these teams, he reminded me. We play each of these teams 14 times over a 70-game schedule. If you want to give it back to somebody, you might want to exercise a little patience and pick your spot. I told Glenn that I had to establish myself, or else. He told me to calm down. Just relax.

Unfortunately, I didn't only take out my aggression on other players. I occasionally felt I had to vent to the referees, too.

And when I gave them some lip, I would get a 10-minute misconduct. I thought I was helping the team by being macho. I wasn't, of course, but I guess my attitude was an extension of what I had gone through the first 19 or 20 years of my life. I figured I had to fight for everything. Back home, one of the kids I fought with was my own size and my own age. But he had three big brothers. The NHL was like that. You might get into it with a guy your size, but that guy had teammates who were bigger than him and bigger than me. When I was growing up, if the big brothers showed up to protect the guy I was fighting, I could always take off and outrun them. That didn't work so well in pro hockey.

At any rate, I was a hellion as a rookie. I didn't fully grasp what Hall meant about calming down until I had my first encounter with Gordie Howe. We were playing the Red Wings and the two of us were scuffling for the puck in the corner. I went to lift up his stick and I missed it. The toe of my blade glanced off his glove and caught him on his cheek, right under his eye. He started bleeding and wiped it off with his finger. Then he looked around to see who did it. Naturally, because I thought I was God's gift to hockey, I yapped at him. I had a smirk on my face and said something about how he was an old man who didn't belong on the ice. Something real smart. Me and my big mouth. We went into the locker room for intermission after the period ended, and Lindsay came over to talk to me. "Maybe you shouldn't have done that," he said. Lindsay knew all about Howe, of course, because they had been teammates in Detroit. "What do you mean?" I said. "Don't you know who that is?" he said. I told Ted that it was an accident. I didn't mean to cut the great Gordie Howe. "No," said Lindsay. "I don't mean that. I mean the way you were talking to him. Maybe you shouldn't have done that."

I thought about what Lindsay said. Maybe I really screwed up. But then I figured, ah, the hell with it, Howe will forget what happened. Big mistake.

As Hall had told me, hockey players wait and pick their spot, and later on that season, Gordie Howe picked his. We were crossing paths at center ice, and the next thing I knew, I

I thought about what Lindsay said. Maybe I really screwed up. But then I figured, ah, the hell with it, Howe will forget what happened. Big mistake.

was down on all fours. My head hurt and I didn't know what had hit me. Amazingly, nobody seemed to know what had hit me, including the referee. I hobbled over to the bench, seeing stars the whole time, when I felt a couple sets of arms under my armpits. I was thrown back onto the ice by a couple guys, who said, "Go back with your own team." Those couple guys were Gordie's teammates. I was so dazed, I had tried to sit down on the wrong bench. I finally made it over to our bench. I still don't know if it was Gordie's elbow or his bare hand. But I know how I felt. In those days, they used to say you had your bell rung. Nowadays, it might be called a concussion. Anyway, I was back taking my regular shift before long and I needed no further introductions to Gordie Howe. I was well acquainted with him at that point.

As I mentioned, I also had some run-ins with the officials. One night, I got called for a penalty by referee Vern Buffey. I didn't care for it, so I charged after him. I meant to stop, but I got my skate caught in the ice and wound up falling into him. In the process, my stick grazed Buffey's body and he immediately hit me with a game misconduct. You don't touch an official,

and I knew I was in trouble. That's a definite no-no, in any era, in any sport. The procedure in those days was that the next time your team went to Montreal for a game, you would visit with NHL president Clarence Campbell at league headquarters. When my time came, I was petrified. Fortunately, two of my teammates went with me—Lindsay and Ed Litzenberger, our captain. They wanted to make sure I didn't say anything stupid. I hope they didn't think I would go after Campbell, too. Campbell didn't object to them accompanying me, but he still gave me a strong lecture, along with a $300 fine, which was a significant amount of money. I left his office with my tail between my legs. I didn't mean to strike Buffey, but I did by mistake and I paid for it, as I should have.

I made some good friends during my first full year with the Blackhawks. I lived with Bobby Hull, Ron Murphy, and Tod Sloan in a two-room apartment in Berwyn, a western suburb that was near an expressway that led to the Stadium. Bobby and I shared a room, Sloan and Murphy were in another, and we each chipped

in $50 for a 1949 Chevy that had a hole in the floor, just in case we wanted to stay cool during the Chicago winters. The heater didn't work, of course, but those were our wheels and we got where we had to go. Bobby and I were single, so we hung out together. Bobby was young and handsome so he didn't have any trouble meeting people, if you know what I mean. I socialized a fair bit too, and I wouldn't say that I exactly roomed with Bobby's suitcase. He was around quite a bit. Murphy and Sloan were married but their families stayed back home in Canada during the season. I likened myself to Sloan as a player. He was a very smooth skater. He looked like a swan out there, skating circles around everybody. If I could be that good out there, I would be happy.

To pass the time, Sloan and another of our teammates, Earl Balfour, went to the racetrack on occasion. I tagged along every once in a while, not knowing anything about horses. But they did, and they also knew a horse that belonged to our owner, James Norris Jr. One day, the boss had a horse named Count Swedak running in the third race. Sloan and Balfour got word from Norris' runner that Norris liked the horse, so they bet on him. Naturally, so did I. I put $50 down on Count Swedak, the most I ever had wagered, and the horse won. I collected $200 and felt like a real expert. I wasn't smart enough to stop there, however, and before my day at the track was over, I ran into an ex-jockey who recognized me as a hockey player. He asked me how much cash I was carrying. I told him about $1,000. He told me about a horse that "couldn't lose" unless it broke a leg or got shot running around the track. I gave him $800 and the horse finished sixth.

The veterans treated us well when they were hazing us or having us do errands, and no veteran was nicer to me than Glenn Hall.

"It stepped in a hole," explained my tipster. "I've got another horse for you. How much money do you have left?"

I gave him $200, and I never saw that again either. When Sloan and Balfour heard about my expensive habit, they laughed about it. They also decided they wouldn't let me out of their sight just in case I had any other ideas. There were a couple other rookies on the team, Bill Hay and Murray Balfour, but I don't recall them ever throwing away money at the track like I did.

The veterans treated us well when they were hazing us or having us do errands, and no veteran was nicer to me than Glenn Hall.

Glenn and his wife, Pauline, that is. She was an absolute queen, not because she was married to a goalie but because she was the sweetest person you would ever want to meet. They had children of their own, but Pauline was like the house-mother to all the young players on the team, particularly me. She was forever inviting me over to the house for dinner, which I appreciated. I ate her food and helped with the dishes but it was more than that. I felt like I was part of a family, and Glenn was a big part

of that, too. I could always talk to him about anything, whether it had to do with hockey or not. Glenn was very wise on a number of issues and also very funny. He had a terrific dry wit that could break the tension in a locker room or anywhere else. The guys loved him, and not only because he could stop pucks with the best of them.

We did show some progress during 1959–60. The Blackhawks made the playoffs in 1960 for a second straight year, which was an accomplishment. In 1959, the year I played just three games for them, they made the playoffs for the first time since 1953, which had marked the first time they qualified since 1946. So you can see why hockey had been down for so long in Chicago and almost out. It's hard to believe now, but during the mid-1950s, the Blackhawks were in so much trouble there actually was talk of them moving to another city, maybe St. Louis. In fact, the Blackhawks played a few "home" games in other places, like St. Louis and even Omaha, Nebraska, if you can believe that. But in 1952, Bill Tobin finally gave up his ownership of the franchise and sold it to James Norris Sr. and Arthur

Wirtz. They owned the Stadium and had lots of money. Norris also owned the Red Wings. He died shortly after the change in ownership and his son, James Jr., took his place in trying to resurrect the Blackhawks along with Wirtz. They hired Tommy Ivan, who had been a very successful coach in Detroit, to run the Blackhawks.

I believe it was Norris Jr. who said, "I can lose $1 million a year and I won't run out of money for two or three centuries."

Ivan was permitted to dip into that reservoir. He bought players, and entire teams, such as the Buffalo farm club that also included the St. Catharines junior club. That's where I was, although I had no idea of the machinations taking place on the business end of the organization. But with a feeder system in place, the Blackhawks eventually landed some good players, and I guess I was one of them. I know Bobby Hull was. In 1959–60, we finished third in the regular season with a record of 28–29–13. We were no match for Montreal in the playoffs,

though. The Canadiens swept us in four games on their way to another Stanley Cup.

At the end of my rookie year, in the spring of 1960, I went back home to Czechoslovakia for the first time since I had left. I had kept in touch with my parents and had sent them money here and there. Not much, just a little. I went with Anna, my mother from Canada, and Irene. Joe, my father in Canada, stayed home. He said somebody had to work. Naturally, I was excited to see my blood parents after all those years and they were excited to see me. The first thing they asked me was whether I was angry or bitter that they had let go of me when I was only eight years old. I said no, of course not. And I was being totally honest. I realized that leaving the old country had opened up my life and allowed me the opportunity to play hockey for a living.

The next thing my blood parents told me was a shocker. They told me to watch what I said to my brother George and sister Viera, who had been born after I left. I'd never seen her. I didn't understand what my parents meant. Then they told me. They weren't sure whether they were members of the Communist party! I was flabbergasted. My own brother and sister, members of the Communist party? I was pretty sure they weren't, but it was quite a jolt. Plus, the entire time I was in Czechoslovakia, I was being followed. That I knew for sure. Wherever I went, I knew I was being tailed.

The people over there knew who I was and what I did. They weren't supposed to know that I played hockey for the Chicago Blackhawks, but even under the suffocating rule of Communism, word spread about things in the world beyond.

My brother set up a gathering of children in the area, a question-and-answer session for lack of a better term. It was quite amusing. One of the first questions I got was "How much money

At training camp before the 1960–61 season, I don't recall us having any great expectations.

do you make?" So, even the kids over there who weren't supposed to know who I was and what I did had an idea. I never answered the question directly. But I did say, "Look, we all eat bread. If I am the lowest-paid worker in North America and I work an hour, I can buy four loaves of bread with what I earned." I don't know how many hours it took to afford four loaves of bread in Czechoslovakia, but it was certainly more than an hour. Obviously, I wasn't the lowest-paid worker in North America, but I didn't want to get into that because I was almost ashamed of what I was making compared with what I knew was going on in Czechoslovakia. I also told the kids that I had to get a job during the summer when I wasn't playing hockey. Just as I once had, those kids thought that there were money trees in North America. Before I left for Canada with Joe, I remember my parents in Czechoslovakia getting mail from him. He would put a $5 bill in there, along with a couple sticks of gum. That was a real treat, being given a stick of gum.

We were over there for about three weeks in 1960. It was quite an education. I recall following my parents' advice for a couple days: I watched what I said. But then I figured that this was my brother and sister. I can't talk to them freely? I can't tell them what's going on in my life? I never did actually ask George or Viera whether they were members of the Communist party, but looking back, I felt I didn't have to ask. They didn't say or do anything to make me suspicious. I went back to the old country several times during my career and my mom came over to the United States on several occasions, but my dad never saw me play a game in the NHL, which I regret. Thankfully, he was around for the 1960–61 season, which was one of the greatest in franchise history and a winter I will never forget.

〰〰〰

At training camp before the 1960–61 season, I don't recall us having any great expectations.

I do remember that we had some veterans on the team who had been in Chicago for a few years and maybe were beginning to see the light. You have to realize that for the longest time, being sent to the Blackhawks meant you were being punished. Hall said when he was traded to Chicago from Detroit that he felt he was going to hockey's Siberia. I don't think the fans in Chicago were convinced we had a great roster, despite the fact that we were coming off two straight playoff appearances. One key acquisition was Ab McDonald, who joined the Blackhawks in a huge nine-player deal with Montreal that also brought us Reggie Fleming, a tough guy. McDonald had won multiple Cups with the Canadiens, so he knew what it took. In my rookie year, I was on a line mostly with Lindsay on the left and Kenny Wharram on the right. Lindsay was near the end of his career and in fact retired after the 1959–60 season, although he gave it one more try four years later in Detroit. I told you he was a tough customer.

McDonald brought a certain leadership to our club. He would speak up whenever he had something to say, even if it meant speaking up to the coach. And I think Rudy appreciated that, up to a point. Ab and I wound up on the same line with Wharram, and Ivan was the first, I believe, to tag us as the "Scooter Line" because we scooted around so much. By this time, I had moved in with Litzenberger and Glen Skov in Glenview, a northern suburb. Litzenberger had endured a terrible tragedy. His wife had been killed in an automobile accident, and Ivan thought it would be a good thing if he lived with a couple guys, which was fine by me.

I was still the kid, so it was my job on occasion to do the cooking. On one cold night, I put three frozen steaks on the outdoor barbeque, left to go inside to get warm, and when I came back, there was a quarter inch of charcoal on the burned side of the steaks.

I served the meal to my roommates, and Litzenberger almost broke his teeth when he bit into the hard side of the steaks. He suggested I throw out the steaks and go buy three more. I don't recall doing much of the cooking after that.

**The original Scooter Line:
Kenny Wharram, yours truly,
and Ab McDonald**

In fact, a couple days later, a kid came knocking on our door looking for work. He was younger than I was, and he became our valet, our handyman. We bought an old car and he was our chauffeur. He also wound up cooking some meals for us. We gave him a few bucks every so often, but only a few. If we made him rich, he wouldn't come back. I think his name was George. Nice fellow, very reliable. He didn't live with us, but he was there whenever we needed him, including pickups at the airport when we came back to Chicago after a road game.

Even though I wasn't living with McDonald, I spent a lot of free time with him. We had a lot of lunches after practice. Kenny would come once in a while, but his wife didn't drive, so he had a lot of responsibilities. So for our lunches, it was mostly Ab and me and a dear friend of mine, Irv Tiahnybik, who owned Leon's Polish Sausage in Chicago. I listened a lot, and Irv was a big help. He had season tickets and knew the game, so I appointed him as my personal scout. He would go to all the home games and then report back to me about what I was doing

wrong. We would get together at a place called Barney's and have our lunches, at least twice a month. Irv sat right behind one net and he would watch the odd road game on TV, so he had plenty of material. And he wasn't afraid to let me know what he thought. Ab, meanwhile, was full of ideas and would actually draw plays up on cocktail napkins. Irv wasn't bashful. After a couple martinis, he might look over to me and say, "Stan, you're not skating worth a damn." (I did mention that we washed down our lunches with adult beverages, didn't I?) I didn't especially like what I was hearing, but I took it to heart. He was a good man and he meant well. Besides, he made a lot of sense. If he said that I was drifting when I skated in over the blue line, maybe he was right.

Ab had theories about how to back check, how to carry the puck into a zone, and anything else that would help us play together. The more we knew about what the other guys on our line were going to do and where they would be, the better chance we had to succeed. If I was in a certain position on the ice (or the cocktail napkin), he would tell me to shoot instead of pass because he would be in the perfect position (elsewhere on the cocktail napkin) for a rebound. Or, he'd suggest that when we enter the opposing zone, I should try a drop pass to Kenny just at the blue line, then cut across to get in position in case Kenny shoots it or passes it to Ab for a shot. We also talked about "coming from behind," or hanging onto the puck until Kenny busted in from right wing. If a defenseman followed Wharram, then I could carry the puck in for a shot or deal it to Ab. It doesn't sound complicated, I know, and it wasn't. But the premise was sound. The three of us needed to be thinking on the same page and playing accordingly. Instinct would take over because each of us had a sense of where the other two guys were and what their next move would be.

Hockey is a freelance game, a game of mistakes. It's not like football where every player on the offensive line and in the backfield has a specific assignment.

But even from a standing start, you can develop a flow in hockey and try to have some sort of idea of what you want to do.

"And we've got to communicate," Ab stressed. "Not only off the ice, on the ice. We need to talk to each other out there, yell at each other." Indeed, I heard him shout "'Kita!" a whole lot. We wound up being a pretty good unit, and I started to score more regularly. During one stretch in late December and early January, I scored 10 goals over eight games. That coincided with a seven-game winning streak for our team that began on Christmas night in Detroit. Not only did we play on Christmas back then, we played on Christmas Eve. We lost in Montreal on Christmas Eve, in fact, and then began our streak the next night. It finally came to an end in Toronto, where I was feeling some pressure to score in a ninth straight game. I didn't sleep well the night before, and then I must have had a dozen shots on Johnny Bower, the Maple Leafs' goalkeeper, but couldn't get anything past him.

Somewhere along the line that season, Ab said something to me that caught my attention.

"You know," he said, "we can go all the way with this team. We can win the Stanley Cup."

I'm not sure if he wrote that on a cocktail napkin, but as I told you, he wasn't afraid to tell you what was on his mind. And if Ab McDonald, who had come to Chicago from a championship team, thought we had enough talent to become one, well, I had to listen. I know one thing. We were a better team than the year before, and a tougher team. Fleming and Murray Balfour didn't take any guff from anybody, and that attitude spread throughout our locker room. We had one particular incident in Toronto that exemplified our one-for-all mind-set.

Pierre Pilote, our great defenseman who was about my size, cracked Eddie Shack of the Maple Leafs over the head with his stick. Before I knew it, Murray was going after Carl Brewer, their defenseman, and chasing him all over the ice. Eventually, Brewer left the rink and started climbing up the stairs by the benches. Balfour went into the stands after him, grabbed him by the ankles, and dragged him down the stairs. Balfour was just about ready to clock Brewer when a guy jumped out of his seat in the stands and went after Balfour. As it turned out, the guy trying to keep Balfour from punching

Brewer happened to be Dick Shatto, who played football with the Toronto Argonauts. So, I went into the stands to help Balfour by going after Shatto. Balfour proceeded to beat the crap out of Brewer, a terrific player but a guy who couldn't fight. Pretty soon the cops arrived to break things up. When it was all over, the referee, Frank Udvari, dished out penalties that resulted in pretty substantial fines. I was really impressed. Here we were in an opposing rink, and we were showing that nobody was going to take advantage of the Blackhawks, especially Blackhawks who weren't very big, like Pilote and me. Another Toronto player, Kent Douglas, didn't forget about that incident and introduced himself to me at a later date. We got tangled up during a game and I just happened to look up when his stick was heading my way. He had the biggest damn handle on that thing.

I closed my eyes and hoped I was having a nightmare, but it was real. I needed about 35 stitches, and I don't believe he even got a penalty.

We finished the regular season with a 29–24–17 record, good for 75 points, which was the first winning record for the Blackhawks since 1945–46. We wound up in third place for the third straight year, 17 points behind the first-place Canadiens, who were seeking their sixth consecutive Stanley Cup. I had 19 goals and 34 assists for 53 points and "only" 100 penalty minutes. Hay led our team in scoring with 59 points, Bobby led the team in goals with 31, and my linemates did well, too. Ab had 17 goals and Kenny scored 16. I wanted badly to reach the 20-goal mark because that was considered pretty hallowed ground. A 20-goal scorer back in the Original Six era was like a .300 hitter in baseball, but it just didn't happen for me that year. Pilote and Moose Vasko were our horses on a defense that also included Al Arbour, who wore glasses when he played. Al, of course, went on to become a great coach with the New York Islanders.

Besides Ab and a few of other true believers, I don't think there were too many people who expected us to get past the Canadiens in the first round. They were loaded and we were just starting to come into our own. The Canadiens

won the first game in the Forum 6–3 but three of their players—Beliveau, Bill Hicke, and Donnie Marshall—got hurt to varying degrees. We started hearing accusations about "dirty hockey," but I thought our style as something else. We were tough and had a certain glue that kept us together. We won the second game in Montreal 4–3 when Litzenberger scored with 2:55 left in the third period. Bobby, Wharram, and I had scored earlier. The series was tied 1–1 and that set the stage for one of the greatest games in team history on March 26, 1961. Fans were beginning to take notice of our team and the Stadium was packed for Game 3 of the best-of-seven semifinals.

The Canadiens had a world of speed and skill, but we were up 1–0 late in a tight-checking game when I got into a fight with Hicke. When we went to the penalty box, we resumed fighting. Penalty boxes are separate now. They weren't then. Hicke and I were separated only by the guy who opened the door. So the referee, Dalton McArthur, hit us each with a five-minute penalty, plus a 10-minute misconduct. We both went downstairs to our locker rooms. I figured the game was about over, and we were going to win. I was preparing to shower and get dressed when I heard this noise from upstairs. Unfortunately, it was not a cheering sound but more like a groan. Sure enough, Henri Richard had scored a goal in the last minute to tie the game 1–1. When my teammates came down for the intermission, I could see they were not too happy. Neither was Pilous, who said to me, "You better get dressed again. We might need you before the night's over."

I still had a lot of penalty time left, so I really didn't think I'd get to play again. But I did, late in the first scoreless overtime period. The second overtime period also was scoreless, although both teams had shots that banged off posts. That just added to the tension, and there was plenty of that in the old building, believe me. It was a warm night to begin with, and most of the fans were in shirtsleeves. The ice was on the soft side, but the mood was heated. McArthur whistled a bunch of penalties in what

was a chippy game, and in the third overtime, he sent Dickie Moore of the Canadiens off for tripping. Rudy sent me out to play the point. Normally, being a right-handed shot, I would have been on the right side. But somehow I ended up on the left side. I got the puck and faked one of their players down as he sort of slid by me. I then shot the puck and Murray Balfour was standing to the left of the Montreal net as I was looking at it. The puck kind of fluttered.

I didn't get much steam on it, but it went right toward Murray, who backhanded the puck past Jacques Plante in the 53rd minute of overtime to give us a 2–1 victory.

The crowd went nuts, and so did Toe Blake, the Montreal coach. He was already angry about the series because he said we should have been

69

I don't want to say our series against Detroit
was anticlimactic, but I will say we never
doubted what the outcome would be.

using tomahawks instead of sticks. So when the Canadiens lost while they were shorthanded, he went onto the ice and took a swing at McArthur. He got a piece of the referee and a piece of Clarence Campbell's mind. Blake was fined $2,000. I vaguely remember Blake first grabbing a chair he was so mad, but he never did throw it. Instead he just made a beeline for McArthur. I can understand why Blake was so furious. Normally, the tripping call on Moore would have been appropriate there. But in the third overtime of a playoff game, I think it could have been overlooked. Not that we were complaining. We were completely sapped after that game.

The episode with Blake was somewhat funny to us, but the main thing is that we had won and we had the Canadiens thinking. They were exhausted too, although they came back in Game 4 at the Stadium with 60 shots on Glenn Hall and won going away 5–2. It was as loud in that building as I ever remember, even though the Canadiens put it to us pretty good. But those were the last goals they scored in the series. Hall shut out the Canadiens 3–0 in Montreal. McDonald, who had missed the start

of the series because of a wrist infection, scored along with Moose Vasko and myself. In Game 6 back at the Stadium, Hall again blanked the Canadiens 3–0 as we got all our goals from the line of Hull, Hay, and Eric Nesterenko. We had won the series much to the surprise of the Canadiens, the entire NHL and all of Canada, which would not have a team in the Stanley Cup Finals because Detroit, which finished fourth in the standings, upset the Toronto Maple Leafs, who had come in second, in five games.

After preventing the heavily favored Canadiens from winning a record sixth straight Cup, we felt pretty good about ourselves.

I don't want to say our series against Detroit was anticlimactic, but I will say we never doubted what the outcome would be.

We had been taking the body pretty well against the Canadiens with guys like Reggie and Jack Evans, and we carried that style into the series against the Red Wings, who had a lot of talent but were not as deep as Montreal. Bobby scored two goals in Game 1 at the Stadium and we won 3–2. Terry Sawchuk, Detroit's goalie, got injured early and was replaced by Hank

Bassen. He started Game 2 in Detroit, which we lost 3–1. We split the next two games, winning 3–1 at the Stadium and losing 2–1 in the Olympia with Sawchuk back in goal for the Red Wings.

In Game 5 at the Stadium, Murray and I each scored two goals in a 6–3 victory. Then in Game 6 at the Olympia, we were down 1–0 when Fleming tied it on a shorthanded goal—a huge momentum swing at that point. If the Red Wings had scored on their power play, it would've been 2–0 and we might have been headed to a Game 7. Instead, we got the next one when Bobby barreled into Bassen, who was back in the net for Detroit because Sawchuk was still bothered by a shoulder injury. Bobby lost control of the puck, but Bassen was down and Ab McDonald had what amounted to a tap-in for the go-ahead goal. We were up 2–1, and then we scored three more in the third

period for a 5–1 win in the game, a 4–2 victory in the series, and the Blackhawks' first Stanley Cup since 1938.

When I look back at those playoffs, I have to say the Montreal roster was scary—Plante, Beliveau, Richard, Moore, Boom Boom Geoffrion, Doug Harvey, Tom Johnson. Talk about a Hall of Fame gathering. Maurice "Rocket" Richard had retired, but Beliveau and Geoffrion finished first and second in the league scoring race while Moore and Henri Richard were also in the top 10. But we believed in ourselves, and a lot of our confidence stemmed from the man in our net—Glenn Hall, Mr. Goalie. He was fabulous, yielding just 27 goals in 12 games, and only 12 in the six games against Detroit. I can't say enough about him. And the fact that he won a Cup in Detroit against a Red Wings team that traded him away had to make it even more special for him.

I had six goals in 12 games, five assists, and only 21 penalty minutes, but I wasn't concerned with personal statistics and I certainly couldn't have been counting the money that I made from winning the Cup. The playoff shares weren't what they are now, but as Glenn used

to say, the owners didn't pay us much, but little did they know we would have played for nothing. That's how much we loved to play. At that stage in my career, I never thought of myself as a celebrity or anything like that. I just happened to be playing games for a living along with a bunch of guys who were as devoted and fortunate as I was.

We carried Glenn off the ice that night—April 16, 1961—and we had a few beers in the dressing room. Then we headed for the airport to catch a commercial flight. We didn't have charters in those days. We didn't even know what a charter was. Jim Norris Jr. made sure we got whatever we wanted at the bar, and we used the hat of Michael Wirtz, one of Arthur's sons, as a champagne glass. There was a snowstorm going on, and eventually our flight to Chicago was cancelled. So we headed back to downtown Detroit, where Norris had lined up a ballroom at the Leland Hotel for us to continue our party. And continue it we did, until maybe 5:00 in the morning or so. Then we went back to the airport for an early morning flight to O'Hare, where a lot of Blackhawks fans greeted us along with fire trucks and a police escort courtesy of Mayor Richard Daley, who later welcomed us to City Hall and proclaimed us "the greatest hockey team ever put together anyplace in this world." Then we adjourned to the Palace Theater to party some more. I don't think I got much sleep, but I was young and excited and I had all summer to rest.

At that age, after only two full seasons with the Blackhawks, I thought winning the Stanley Cup would be a common occurrence. I figured we would at least win multiple Cups over a period of a few years. Maybe two in three years, four in six years, something like that. I've talked with Bobby over the years about it and he felt the same way. Little did we know that we would not be so fortunate. Hockey had become huge in Chicago after a long, dark period, and with the team we had, I thought we would win it all over and over again. I thought we had the secret. I thought we were a dynasty. I only wish that was true. I never won another Stanley Cup with the Blackhawks.

At the time, even though it was a great thrill, I didn't fully grasp what it meant to win the Stanley Cup. But the longer I went without

winning again, the more I realized how difficult it is to win even one. That's what I took with me into retirement, and that's a message both Bobby and I tried to convey to the Blackhawks in 2010. They had a lot of kids, like Bobby and I were in 1961, and we just wanted to relay what we had experienced. You never know when you are going to get another chance. You never know *if* you will get another chance. So make the most of it. The Blackhawks did in 2010, bringing the Stanley Cup back to Chicago for the first time since we did in 1961. It was a thrill to watch them play and be around for the celebrations.

Hockey was pretty big in Chicago when I played, but when I saw the size of the parade for the 2010 team, I was amazed. The city estimated that 2 million people showed up in the Loop. I guess that disproves the theory about how there are only 18,000 hockey fans in Chicago, doesn't it?

Top row: Nick Garen (trainer), Murray Balfour, Pierre Pilote, Chico Maki, Stan Mikita, Ron Murphy, Wayne Hicks, Tod Sloan, Kenny Wharram, Walter Humeniuk (equipment mgr. and spare goalie); Middle row: John P. Gottselig (dir. of publicity), Eric Nesterenko, Dollard St. Laurent, Earl Balfour, Elmer Vasko, Ab McDonald, Al Arbour, Jack Evans, Wayne Hillman, Michael Wirtz (vice president); Bottom row: Glenn Hall, Ed Litzenberger, Reg Fleming, Arthur M. Wirtz (president), Thomas N. Ivan (general manager), James D. Norris (chairman), Rudy Pilous (coach), Bobby Hull, Red Hay, Denis DeJordy

It happened by accident, during just another scrimmage. We were practicing at the Stadium early in my career with the Blackhawks. I got the puck in our zone and started to carry it up along the right boards. I was checked into the door that opens and closes to the players' bench, and my stick got caught in the crack of the doorway. Because I was still moving and the stick was imbedded, something had to give. I heard a crunching noise, and then I let go of the stick. When I went back to retrieve it, I noticed that the blade had been bent slightly. It had a curve, like a banana.

I used to bring only one stick with me to practice, and because we were near the end of our scrimmage, I didn't bother to go get another one. So, I kept playing with the one I had. Before I left the ice, I saw a puck just laying there and I took a shot with the curved stick. I felt a different sensation. The puck not only sounded different, but it acted different coming off that curved blade. I took a few more shots with a few more pucks. Same thing. Interesting.

When I went downstairs after practice, I looked for my supply of spare sticks. I had about a dozen in reserve. I decided to do some experimenting. How could I bend the blade on a few of those spares? I first tried to bend them under the door. I cracked the first one. Those sticks were pretty solid. Wait a minute. My dad, Joe, was a carpenter. If he wanted to bend wood, what would he do? He would heat up the wood, which is what I did. I stuck it under the hot water in the sink, and after a few minutes, it bent. Then I stuck it under cold water, and the curve held its position. By the next morning, the stick was firm, and the curve was there. Water hadn't affected the blade, which was laminated.

I continued to fiddle with the curved stick, usually by myself, shooting pucks before and after practice. Again, the pucks came off at different angles and with more velocity than they would with a straight blade. I play golf, and when you hit an iron shot, you want to make a descending blow into the ball, also hitting the ground just behind it. I took a slap shot using the same method in hockey, by striking the ice surface just behind the puck. You are essentially de-lofting the club, or stick. I was taught to take the weight off my back foot and shoot off the front foot, leaning forward, to create a bow-and-arrow effect.

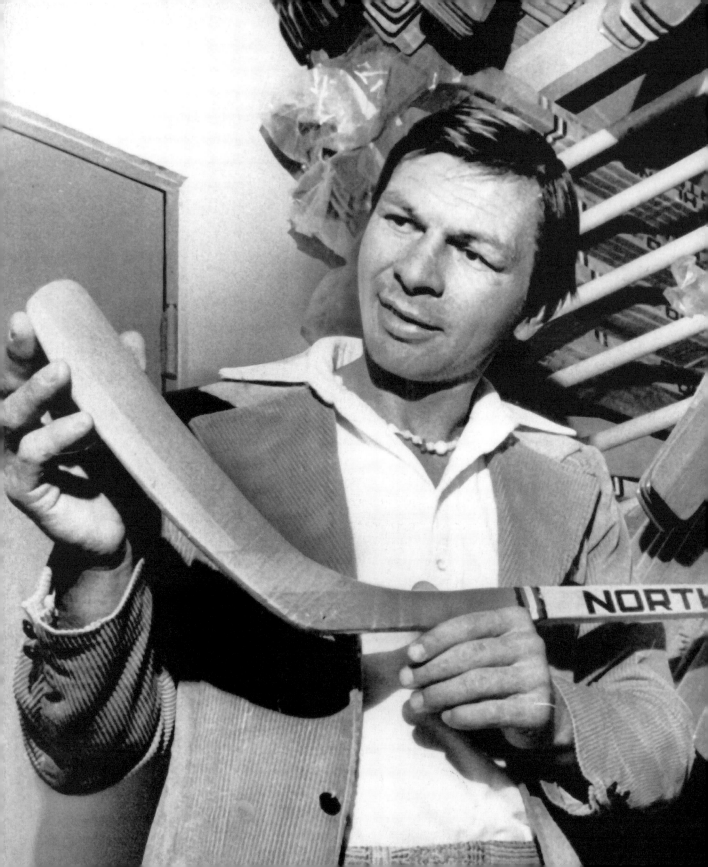

That motion worked great with the curved blade. For a month or so, I toyed with it pretty much in secret. But one day, Bobby Hull came early to the Stadium, and he said, "I think I caught you." I said, "I guess you did." I talked to him about the curved blade, and he wanted me to help make him one. Eventually, we wound up using the hydrocollator that trainers had for physical therapy. You could heat up a blade in a hurry with those. It would come out looking like spaghetti after a minute. Then we'd put the blade in a bucket of ice to make it solid. Then we tried the torch that trainers used. Understand that there was no manual on curved blades. There were no rules against them, either. Every day was a new day of experimentation. Eventually, we latched onto the propane gas torch that trainers carried around.

You should have seen Bobby Hull's first shot with the curved blade! He was a lot stronger than I was, and that puck really flew. The curved blade did affect my backhand. As a center, I had a right wing to think of, so I continued to play with the blade. If it was 12 inches long, I would have it straight for about nine inches starting with the heel so I could still pass the puck on the backhand, and then the last three inches by the toe would be curved, like a cradle.

Bobby and I started using curved sticks in games, and the idea did not go over well with goalies. It was tough enough for them to stop Bobby without the curved stick. But when he started hitting pucks that had a mind of their own, goalies became a bit upset. Ed Giacomin of the New York Rangers was one of them, and he went to the league to complain that something had to be done. My shot would not break a pane of glass even with the curved blade, but it did do tricks with the curved blade, which might have contributed to a generation of youngsters who were in love with the slap shot and never used the backhand.

In the late 1960s, the NHL wrote a rule restricting the extent to which a stick could be curved. Oddly enough, during the 1972 Stanley Cup playoffs against the Pittsburgh Penguins, Dennis Hull had his stick confiscated during a game, after which it was found to be curved three-eighths of an inch over the legal limit of a half inch. He was fined, and there was even talk that the Blackhawks would refuse to play the rest of the games. We never did go on strike. Much ado about nothing.

Many years later, Andy Bathgate spoke out and said he invented the curved stick. He said he was using them in the 1960s when he was a kid in Winnipeg, and then played with them as a member of the New York Rangers. He claimed I stole his idea. He said he thought he saw me one day in their locker room at Madison Square Garden, looking over his sticks. This was in 1999, almost 20 years after I retired, when he came out with this. I like Andy. We're friends. I never said, "I alone invented the curved stick." I never took credit for anything. I never said I was Thomas Edison. But I do know that after Bobby and I started playing with them, the curved sticks turned up everywhere around the NHL, and they're still there today.

"I guarantee you, if you had placed a wager during my first few seasons in the NHL that I would someday be hailed for sportsmanship and gentlemanly conduct, you would have gotten some really long odds."

—STAN MIKITA

COMMITTED TO THE INDIAN

One incident that no doubt influenced my career came thanks to our oldest child, Meg, who was watching a game at home on TV before she was even two years old. She might have been only 14 months or so, but she was very attentive and bright, qualities she obviously inherited from her mother. We were playing in New York against the Rangers in 1965, and Jill let her watch the first period before it was time for her to go to bed. Meg was able to walk at eight months, and before too long, she developed a vague idea of what her father did for a living.

I still had a chip on my shoulder at the time, and so I spent a few choice minutes in the Madison Square Garden penalty box, a point Meg picked up on while watching.

"Why," she asked her mother, "does Daddy always sit by himself? Why doesn't he sit with his friends, like Uncle Kenny [Wharram] and Uncle Bobby [Hull]?"

Very perceptive. Of course, the reason was obvious. If you're serving a penalty, you aren't sitting with your teammates on the bench. Her reaction stopped and made me think. If our baby daughter sees this and feels something is wrong, why can't I? Maybe I was spending too much time serving penalties for my own good and for the good of the team.

"You played really well," Meg said when I came through the door. "But why did you have to skate all the way on the other side of your friends to sit alone?"

In my rookie year with the Blackhawks, I accumulated 119 penalty minutes. In 1960–61, the year we won the Cup, I had 100. The next two seasons, I went down to 97 and 69, but in 1963–64, I went back up to 146 and in 1964–65, I was up to 154. You can do the math. A hockey game is 60 minutes long, so 154 minutes meant I spent almost 2½ hours, or 2½ games, in the box. The year after Meg said her piece, I took only 58 penalty minutes. I'm sure I thought about what she had asked me, and even if it didn't occur to me every day, I did make a conscious effort at least to cut down on the stupid stuff. In other words, misconducts.

First, I stopped mouthing off to referees. At the start of my "transformation," I took a few of the officials by surprise. When they would blow a whistle, they more or less expected me to have something to say. But in my attempt to become a nicer guy, at least to them, I might make eye contact with them and just skate away. I'm sure they were saying, "What's wrong with him? Why is he so quiet all of a sudden?" John Ashley, a referee you could talk to, even came up to me one night and felt my forehead as if to take my temperature.

Another thing I did was make an honest assessment of my behavior on the ice. I studied the score sheets after each game to break down what kind of penalties I was taking. During my days as a hellion, I received a fair share of penalties for high-sticking, slashing, spearing, tripping, and hooking. Those penalties fell under the category of "lazy," because if I had taken another stride or made a little more effort, maybe I wouldn't have had to lay the lumber on a guy to slow him down or stop him. So, in addition to cutting out the stupid infractions such as misconducts, I tried to subtract the "lazies."

Mind you, if I had to chop a guy's arm off to prevent a goal, I would. But how many occasions like that actually present themselves?

Jill also contributed to my rehabilitation act in her own way. She would simply say, "Stan, we're running out of money." A 10-minute misconduct cost $25, and a game misconduct was $100. Those sums were automatically deducted from your paycheck. You never saw the money, and as a result, it seemed that I never saw the same paycheck twice. I noticed that the figures were always different, and so did my lovely wife. She joked that she never knew whether we would be having steak for dinner or hamburger. At least I think it was a joke. We weren't really running out of money, of course, but her point was well taken. I was throwing away a lot of cash, often by trying to referee a game in addition to playing it.

Jill had a great knack for bringing me back to reality. She never let me get too high or too low.

She did say I never brought the game home with me, and Jill didn't comment on how I did in any particular game. One time,

I scored two goals and she said she thought I did really well. I told her it might have been one of the worst games I ever played. "I never said another word after that," she says. When we got into the car after a home game, the discussion was pretty simple. Where is everybody going for a beer?

Lo and behold, I spent only 12 minutes in the penalty box in 1966–67, followed by just 14 the next season. And both of those years, I was honored by winning the Lady Byng Memorial Trophy, an annual award "to the player adjudged to have exhibited the best type of sportsmanship and gentlemanly conduct combined with a high standard of playing ability." How about that, sports fans? I guarantee you, if you had placed a wager during my first few seasons in the NHL that I would someday be hailed for sportsmanship and gentlemanly conduct, you would have gotten some really long odds. But it happened, and it was because I had become a smarter player and also felt a greater sense of responsibility, having married Jill and started a family.

"AT THE START OF MY 'TRANSFORMATION,' I TOOK A FEW OF THE OFFICIALS BY SURPRISE."

—STAN MIKITA

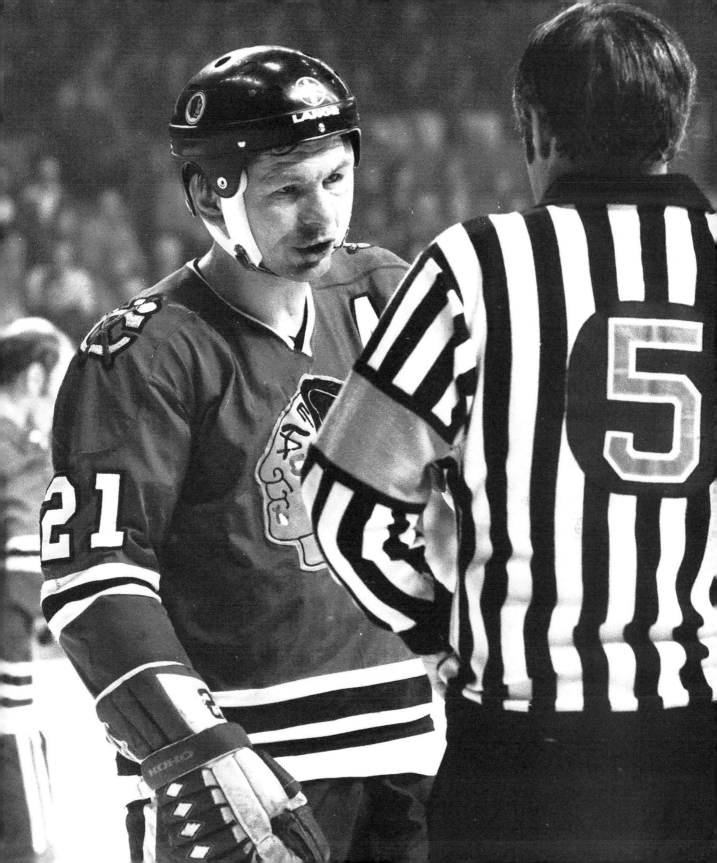

The year after we won the Cup, we still had the nucleus of a terrific team, plus the experience of knowing what it took to win it all. We beat Montreal in six games in the first round of the playoffs, but then we ran into the Toronto Maple Leafs. Under Punch Imlach, their very wily coach, the Leafs had loaded up on older players, and they served him well. They beat us in the Finals 4–2, and that kind of set the tone for what we would encounter in subsequent seasons, even though we had a solid roster. Why we couldn't get over the hump, I wish I knew. Heck, in 1963–64, five of the six first-team NHL All-Stars were Blackhawks—Glenn Hall, Pierre Pilote, Wharram, Hull, and myself. Tim Horton, the Toronto defenseman, was the only other guy on the first team, and Moose Vasko was named to the second All-Star team. Yet, with all that talent, we didn't even finish first in the league.

There was no way to explain it. Before the start of the 1963–64 season, Tommy Ivan made a change behind the bench, firing Rudy Pilous and hiring Billy Reay. That occurred during the spring of 1963, after we had a pretty good regular season but were eliminated in the first round of the playoffs by the Red Wings, who won four straight games after losing the first two. Jill and I were on our honeymoon in Hawaii when the announcement was made. There were no cell phones then, of course, but during our three weeks away, Jill's mother sent us some newspaper clippings from Chicago. Much to my surprise, it was being reported that I was one of the ringleaders in getting Rudy canned. I was sunning myself on the beach with my bride and I'm getting coaches fired? I have no idea where that stuff started, but I do know I never had a bad word to say about Rudy Pilous. I went back a long way with him, to the time I was a kid in St. Catharines. I grew up in his backyard. When I got back to Chicago, I was asked about my role in Rudy's dismissal and I attempted to set the record straight by telling reporters that I had no role whatsoever.

Something must have been going on involving Rudy, but it was something I was completely unaware of. Again, after we won the Cup, expectations were that we would win more than one. The players felt that way, so I imagine the front office thought likewise.

86

When we didn't win another Cup in 1962 or 1963, I guess some restlessness set in. I can't pinpoint the exact time, but there were even rumors circulating that Bobby was going to be traded, or that I was going to be traded, or that we were both on the block. I didn't pay much attention to the reports, but I did get one phone call that shook me during the summer of 1964, after Detroit had knocked us out of the playoffs again in seven games in the first round. Wharram was on the horn from his home in Canada with the news that Ab McDonald, our left winger on the Scooter Line, had been dealt to Boston along with Reggie Fleming for Doug Mohns, a defenseman.

I didn't understand why Ab was traded. Maybe he asked for more money. Probably, he asked for more money. Whatever, it bothered me, and it took Jill and Kenny to remind me that this was a business. Trades happen all the time. Live with it. I really didn't need a lot of convincing that hockey was a business. We were playing in a six-team league, which meant very few NHL jobs, and management had all the leverage. I learned that the year after we won the Cup and Tommy Ivan welcomed me into his office to discuss a new contract.

"My boy," he said, "we are prepared to give you a nice raise for your fine performance. We are prepared to give you a $500 raise." I replied, "Mr. Ivan, when did you become a comedian?"

Tommy didn't think that was very funny. I don't think he appreciated my sense of humor. I had made $8,500 the previous two years, and now I was going to be boosted all the way to $9,000. Tommy justified it by saying that I had gotten a pretty good deal when I signed as a rookie. I countered by saying that I thought I had been a pretty good player on a team that won the Stanley Cup. I had also received a signing bonus along with that first contract, so in effect, I was taking a cut with my second contract, but that's the way it was.

In 1965, after two straight years of leading the league in scoring, I went right down to the

"**THE YEAR AFTER WE WON**
THE CUP, WE STILL HAD THE
NUCLEUS OF A TERRIFIC TEAM,
PLUS THE EXPERIENCE OF KNOWING
WHAT IT TOOK TO WIN IT ALL."

—STAN MIKITA

wire with Tommy. You could report to training camp and play exhibition games without a contract then, and if you happened to get hurt without signing anything, tough luck. We were in Toronto for our regular season opener, I still hadn't signed, and I told Tommy that if we didn't make a deal by 6:00 PM the night before our opener, I was going to leave the hotel and fly back to Chicago.

Sure enough, at 6:00 nothing happened, so I grabbed my bag, went downstairs at the Royal York hotel, and jumped on an airport bus. I could have hailed a taxi, but I was trying to save money. There were only a couple other people on the bus and the driver was all set to leave when a bell boy came outside, banging on the door. He asked the driver, "Is there a Stan Mikita on board?" I was told there was a phone call for me in the lobby. I left the bus, picked up the house phone, and it was Tommy. He wanted me to come up to his room.

When I got there, Tommy asked if I was ready to negotiate a contract. We went around in circles again without making any progress, at which point Tommy called Jim Norris, our owner, in Florida. He was on his boat. Tommy

talked with Norris, then hung up. We can't afford to pay you what you want, Tommy said. But I think we can give you another $250. I grabbed my bag and started to head back downstairs. Tommy stopped me, and then, at my request, he gave me Mr. Norris' phone number. I went downstairs, phoned the boss, and Mr. Norris said, no problem. We'll pay you what you're asking. I remember what Mr. Norris had told me along the way. No matter what happens, kid, you'll be with the Blackhawks for a long time.

I went back upstairs to tell Tommy about my conversation with the boss and signed. I believe my windfall was for $12,500.

During our entire back-and-forth, Tommy kept reminding me of that big raise I'd just hit them up for a few years earlier. The $500 raise. During the course of my career, I had certain bonus clauses built into my contracts, as did most players. But some of those clauses were really crazy. Yeah, if I scored 100 goals in one season, I would have made a killing. You

Me and Blackhawks owner Jim Norris, Jr.

get the idea. If I had made good on some of those bonus clauses, I could have owned the Blackhawks. But Tommy had a budget and he was just trying to do his job. And he did it well.

〰〰〰〰〰

After Ab was traded, Billy Reay tried a couple of pretty good young players, Doug Robinson and John Brenneman, on a line with Kenny and me. Nothing quite clicked, for no particular reason. Then at some point, we noticed how Mohns came storming out of our end. We called him "Dougie the Diesel." He sure looked like he could be a heck of a forward, even if he wasn't in Boston. He had as much speed as Kenny. Like Ab, when Mohns got the puck, it was difficult to take it away from him. When Kenny and I brought the subject up with Reay, he looked at us like we were crazy. But after Mohns was with us for a month or so, he became our left winger and the second Scooter Line was born. I don't know that we were better than the first one, but

The second Scooter Line: Wharram, Mikita, and Mohns

we were at least as good. Mohns could really skate, he could move the puck, and he had a terrific shot. After the three of us became a line during the 1964–65 season, all of us thrived. For the next four years, each of us had at least 20 goals. I don't believe there were any other NHL lines that could match that.

Mohns also contributed, unintentionally, to one of my freakiest of several freaky injuries. We were playing in Pittsburgh in December of 1967, shortly after the Penguins joined the NHL as an expansion team. Mohns fired the puck from inside the blue line and I was standing near their net, waiting for a rebound.

The puck struck a defenseman's stick and deflected toward my head. My first reaction was to duck and protect my eyes, but the puck hit my right ear with a vengeance and almost tore the entire thing off. I didn't realize the extent of the damage until I was dragged to the bench, then the dressing room, by one of our trainers, Socko Uren. When I looked in the mirror, I came very close to passing out. My right ear was hanging from the rest of my head by what seemed to be a thread. It was gruesome, a bloody mess.

Soon, the Penguins' team physician got a hold of me and immediately froze the ear. Then, he miraculously sewed it back into place with a few dozen stitches. Before all this happened, I asked for a phone so I could call Jill. I knew she would have been watching at home, and she was. She was frantic. She thought the puck caught me in the eyes, and when I told her that it hadn't, she calmed down a bit. I didn't think it was necessary to tell her that I had come close to leaving my right ear on the ice.

We flew back to Chicago, where I was sent to Henrotin Hospital. I spent the day there, and around 6:00 or so that night, headed to the Stadium for our next game. I wasn't thinking about playing, but when I got there, I talked to Uren about grabbing a steel cup from an athletic supporter. Maybe we could attach it to a helmet that I had been using on and off to protect me from a few of my other freakish injuries. He wrapped the cup in tape and fit it over my ear without actually touching it. I then went to Reay and said I thought I could play with that contraption.

"What if you get hit in the same place again?" asked Billy, thinking rationally.

"Well, I guess they can sew it up again," I said. So I played, I assisted on a goal by Mohns, and we beat Toronto 2–0. I didn't really make much of the whole episode. I wasn't trying to prove anything, that's for sure. Hockey players have and always have had a history of playing through injuries, possibly out of fear of losing our jobs to someone else, but more likely because that's just part of our work ethic. I'm reminded of Bobby Jones, a great golfer from the old days who called a penalty on himself when nobody else was looking—a common practice in that sport. When someone praised Jones for his honesty, he replied, "That's like congratulating me for not robbing a bank."

In other words, that's what we do as professional athletes. You always hear that hockey players will play with broken bones while baseball players will sit out for days with a hangnail. I can't comment on that because I've never been a professional baseball player. But I have seen teammates and opponents play when they were hurt, really hurt, and if I sat out every time my back bothered me throughout my career, I would have had a sore behind instead. So I wore a brace and even submitted to a series of experimental injections—about 150 over two different sessions from Dr. Gustav Hemwall— to cure the pain. It wasn't acupuncture, but it was similar in that the doctor would insert a needle with dextrose into the problem area, reinjure the scar tissue, then build it back up. I did this procedure on my own, without telling the Blackhawks or anybody else. It was a gamble of sorts, but it was better than having surgery.

I don't mean to make light of injuries. There have been some serious ones over the years. Doug Barkley, an excellent defenseman, caught a stick in the eye and lost his vision. Bill Masterton, who played for the Minnesota North Stars, lost his life in 1968 after being injured in a hockey game. There is a prestigious award in his name given annually to the NHL player who exhibits a high degree of perseverance. What happened to Masterton was a tragedy. What I endured over 22 years was not tragic, only annoying. I hurt just about every part of my body at least once and usually more than once. Thankfully, I'm still able to walk and talk and enjoy my family.

After trying a helmet on and off, I eventually settled on wearing one full time. I had taken a lot of blows to the head, like the one from Kent Douglas. I don't think a helmet would have saved me from almost losing my right ear in Pittsburgh, but gradually I came to realize that I could still play at a high level with headgear on. Red Berenson wore one all the time before me, and it didn't hurt his performance. In some circles, I suppose, wearing a helmet wasn't considered macho. Some guys wouldn't have wanted one because they thought it covered their nice head of hair and destroyed their good looks. I didn't have to worry about my good looks. I didn't have any to destroy. I also didn't worry about being thought of as a chicken, not after some of the hard knocks I had taken. Besides, I was on the ice 24 hours after that

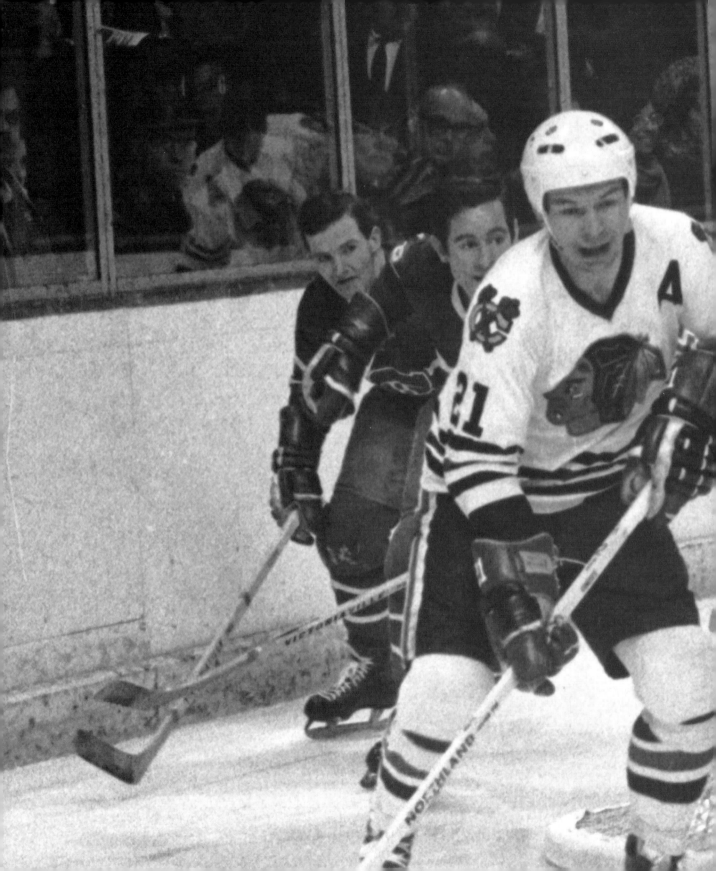

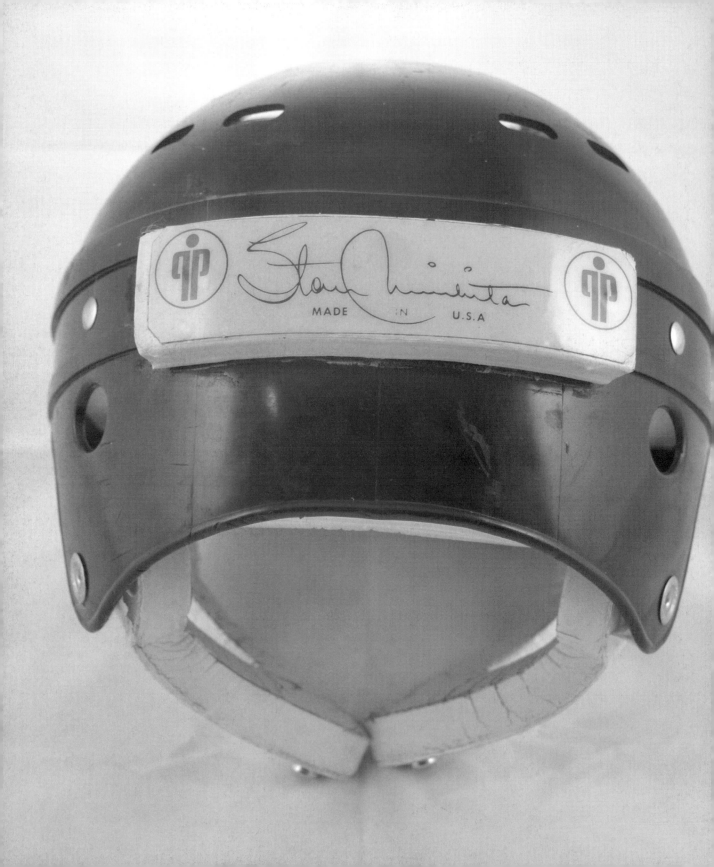

"GRADUALLY, HELMETS WERE ENGINEERED TO BECOME LIGHTER AND BETTER, ALMOST TO THE POINT WHERE YOU DIDN'T REALIZE YOU HAD ONE ON."

—STAN MIKITA

ear injury in Pittsburgh. On one occasion, I heard Claude Ruel, the coach of the Canadiens, screaming for his guys to hit me in the head during a game. I couldn't believe it. Here was a guy who had lost an eye in hockey, and he's urging his guys to be headhunters! The myth that helmets affected your peripheral vision was just that, a myth. At least for me. Gradually, helmets were engineered to become lighter and better, almost to the point where you didn't realize you had one on. Now, of course, all players in the NHL wear helmets. They're mandatory.

It was during the 1966–67 season that I began to hear about "the Curse of Muldoon." I had no idea what it was about, but eventually, you learned it was part of Blackhawks history. Ancient history.

In 1927, only a year after the Chicago franchise was born, the original owner, Major Frederic McLaughlin, fired his coach, Pete Muldoon. McLaughlin made his fortune in other fields, and when he spent a bunch of money for hockey players, he demanded a

lot. When the team he thought should have finished in first place finished in third place, he gave the pink slip to Muldoon, who didn't take too kindly to his dismissal. This team will never finish first, Muldoon warned upon leaving.

Or so goes the story. There is some question about whether it's really true or is one of those tales that grows over time, maybe with a little push from sportswriters. The problem with the Curse of Muldoon was that it seemed to be working because the Blackhawks didn't finish first for 40 years. Even the three seasons when Chicago won the Cup—1934, 1938, and ours in 1961—the team didn't finish first during the regular schedule.

In 1966–67, we had a chance to finish first, and naturally, our friends in the media reminded us about the Curse of Muldoon. But after finishing second the previous year, we had acquired some players who provided us with depth. Dennis Hull, who had been with us before, stayed for the entire season and scored 25 goals. Ed Van Impe, a rugged defenseman who had also been in the system, stuck with us, and so did Lou Angotti. Vasko had retired, but Ivan convinced Bill Hay, who had retired after the 1965–66 season, to make a comeback, and he was a big help when he returned at midseason. Hay didn't need the money. His father was president of an oil company, so the family wasn't hurting. But Ivan convinced him that we needed him, which we did, and Bill was terrific—a leader on and off the ice. Also, we beefed up our goalkeeping by bringing in Denis DeJordy to be Hall's sidekick. The days of teams having only one goalie were over, and pretty soon, so would the six-team league. Expansion was on the horizon.

We marked the occasion by finishing first in the last year of the Original Six era. We won 41 games, lost only 17, and tied 12 for 94 points, 17 more than second-place Montreal. We scored 264 goals, a league record to that point, and yielded only 170, the fewest in the NHL that season. The Curse of Muldoon had been put to rest! We had quite the celebration after clinching on a Sunday afternoon in the Stadium by whipping Toronto 5–0. We tossed Ivan and Reay into the shower while they were wearing very nice suits, if you can imagine that. Grown men acting like boys. But it was a big

deal for us to finish a great regular season in first place, and individually, it was a significant season because I managed to collect the Hart Trophy as the league's most valuable player, the Ross Trophy as the leading scorer, and the Lady Byng Trophy that I previously mentioned.

No player in NHL history ever secured those three honors in the same season, and I would be lying if I said it wasn't a source of personal satisfaction. But our first-place finish represented a group effort. Bobby collected 52 goals, only two fewer than the previous season when he'd scored a record 54, and the Vezina Trophy for goalkeeping honors was shared by Hall and DeJordy. Naturally, we all thought we were primed for a run at the Stanley Cup, but as I look back, maybe the fact that we clinched first place with a few weeks left in the regular season hurt us in the playoffs. We won our opener 5–2 against Toronto at the Stadium. But in Game 2, we ran into Terry Sawchuk, who played a tremendous game in goal. We just couldn't get much past him, and we lost 3–1. He did to us what Glenn Hall had done to the Canadiens when we upset them in 1961. The Maple Leafs beat us in six games, then went

"I DIDN'T HAVE TO WORRY ABOUT MY GOOD LOOKS. I DIDN'T HAVE ANY TO DESTROY. I ALSO DIDN'T WORRY ABOUT BEING THOUGHT OF AS A CHICKEN, NOT AFTER SOME OF THE HARD KNOCKS I HAD TAKEN."

—STAN MIKITA

on to win the Stanley Cup we thought would be ours.

Finishing first was nice, but we didn't finish the job, and that season wound up as a real disappointment. You don't have to play your best during the regular season, to be honest, as long as you make the playoffs, which is when you *do* have to play your best. Maybe we expended so much energy and effort to finish first that we didn't have much left in the tank for the postseason. I don't know. I wish I did know. It did seem as though that Toronto team, and others down the line, had an idea how to play us. The Leafs were physical, experienced, and they checked the hell out of us. They hit everything that moved. They weren't fancy, just very simple.

While the Maple Leafs and Canadiens were headed to the Stanley Cup Finals, I went to Toronto for the awards ceremony. It was a luncheon, and at the time, the only trophy I knew I would win was the Art Ross. I had 35 goals and 62 assists for 97 points, 17 more than Bobby, who was second in the league in scoring.

It was my third Ross in four seasons. I won in 1964 and 1965, and Bobby won in 1966. At the ceremony, I was seated around Harry Howell of the New York Rangers, who would win the Norris Trophy as best defenseman, and Bobby Orr of the Boston Bruins, who would win the Calder Trophy as best rookie. I thought I had a chance at the Lady Byng because of my modest 12 penalty minutes and was pleased when it was announced that I had indeed won it. There was a monetary reward for the Byng of $1,000, which was nice, although it probably didn't cover all the fines I paid before I decided to become an altar boy. Then, when I also received the Hart, I was somewhat shocked. Bobby had won it the previous two years, and when I learned how the voting went—I received 168 out of a possible 180 points, beating out Ed Giacomin, the New York Rangers' fine goalie—I was almost speechless. Almost.

My old friend, NHL president Clarence Campbell, noted that my winning three trophies was quite an accomplishment "for a young man who came from Czechoslovakia." That triggered something in my mind. I thought about Jill and Meg, who had traveled with me

104

to Toronto for the day but weren't permitted to attend the announcement (more about that later). I reviewed in my mind some of the many peaks and valleys I had encountered along the way, from making it to the NHL, then staying in the NHL, then gradually refining my game to become a better player, a smarter player. Or, as Jill likes to say, more mature.

"Well," I said as part of my acceptance speech, "as my wife told me before I walked into this room today, this isn't all bad for a little DP."

It got a good laugh. At that time, 97 points tied the NHL record for most by an individual during a regular season (Bobby had set that record the previous year). Oddly enough, in our final regular season game, I touched the puck before Mohns scored his 25th goal. I thought I deserved an assist, which would have brought my point total to 98, but I wasn't about to make an issue of it. I knew the record I shared of 97 points would be broken sooner rather than later anyway. I was proud of what I had done that season, a season we destroyed the Curse of Muldoon but again came up short in the playoffs.

Despite being awarded the Lady Byng, I had built up my share of grudges, if you want to call them that. Henri Richard and I went at it quite often. Our battles were strictly on the ice. I respected him as a player, and if I didn't, all he had to do was show me his Stanley Cup rings. How many did he wind up with, 11? His brother, Maurice, was also a tremendous player. Then, after he retired, he sat behind the Canadiens' bench in the Montreal Forum and made sure to swear at me in French whenever we came to town. One time, he tossed a cup of something at me. I think it was a Coca-Cola. Very syrupy. Eddie Shack of the Maple Leafs was another tormentor, as was Lou Fontinato of the Rangers.

Then there was Bob Pulford, whom I would encounter many years later when he came to the Blackhawks' front office. As a player in Toronto, he was pretty good with the lumber. He was bigger than me and mean. We didn't wear anything to protect our upper arms back then, and he would always go the extra few strides to let me have it long after I passed or shot the puck. We had our fights, including

"MY OLD FRIEND, NHL PRESIDENT CLARENCE CAMPBELL, NOTED THAT MY WINNING THREE TROPHIES WAS QUITE AN ACCOMPLISHMENT 'FOR A YOUNG MAN WHO CAME FROM CZECHOSLOVAKIA.'"

—STAN MIKITA

one after he went to the Los Angeles Kings. One night in the Forum, we got into it in the penalty box. We were both thrown out of the game, so we went toward our dressing rooms. Before we reached our destinations, we crossed paths and had a stick fight in the hallway. We just couldn't get enough of each other, we were such pals. I didn't think our rivalry would continue, but it did. At least it did from his point of view.

Notice that I have recently referred to teams from Pittsburgh and Los Angeles. In 1967, the NHL underwent a drastic makeover, doubling in size from six to 12 teams. Besides Pittsburgh and Los Angeles, expansion franchises were awarded to Philadelphia, St. Louis, Minneapolis, and Oakland. All six new teams were place in the Western Division, while the Original Six were in the Eastern Division. The impact on the owners was more money via expansion fees—$2 million per franchise—and in order to stock the new clubs, Original Six teams had to make players available through the expansion draft. We lost Angotti, Van Impe, and Mr. Goalie himself, Glenn Hall, whom the Blackhawks left off the protected list

because, I believe, they thought he was going to retire. Glenn frequently talked about quitting, so management took the gamble by making him available. The Blues of St. Louis also took a gamble by selecting him. They paid him more than he'd ever made, he "unretired," and played great for the Blues. He became a hero in St. Louis, where he helped put hockey on the map.

The new era also caused the Blackhawks to make a controversial trade, sending Phil Esposito, Ken Hodge, and Fred Stanfield to Boston for Gilles Marotte, Pit Martin, and Jack Norris. Phil had been the center for Bobby and Chico Maki, so they felt the way I felt after Ab McDonald had been traded away. I had no inside information on why Esposito was traded, other than the persistent talk that our front office felt he wasn't working hard enough. I don't necessarily mean lazy, because he certainly wasn't. It was just Phil's way. He was a big guy who maybe didn't appear to be skating as fast as he could, or whatever. I do know that I was surprised, as were a lot of other people around Chicago. I was not surprised that he caught fire with the Bruins where, along with Bobby Orr, he helped build a team that would soon be formidable. Stanfield was a heck of a player too, and so was Hodge. That was the trade of trades. If we had sent only Esposito to Boston, it wouldn't have been such a good deal for the Blackhawks, and I say that not to disrespect any of the players we acquired. But Phil is in the Hall of Fame.

The Blackhawks acquired Marotte to beef up our defense, and Martin was a center who could take over for Esposito. Norris was a goalie who was supposed to help replace Hall, along with DeJordy and Dave Dryden. As Phil began piling up points, reviews of the trade in Chicago became more critical. Ironically, I wound up in a duel with Phil and Gordie Howe for the scoring title. It went down to the last day. I led Phil by one point and Gordie by three. The Red Wings were beating us 5–4 in the Stadium when I took a pass from Mohns at the right point. I decided to try something I'd been thinking about for years: a lob shot on net. The puck kind of waffled in the air, took a couple of weird hops, and then bounced in past goalie Roger Crozier—just like I planned it. That tied the game at 5–5 and was my 40th goal of the season—the most I ever scored in one

year—and I wound up with 87 points, three more than Phil. I don't know what Chicago fans would have thought if Esposito won a scoring title in his first year after being traded to Boston, but at least I didn't have to worry about it.

We beat the Rangers in the first round of the playoffs, then got knocked out by Montreal in the second round. (The playoffs had expanded to three rounds because the winner of the Western Division automatically got a berth in the Finals against the Eastern champion.) After we were eliminated, our family went to Ft. Lauderdale for vacation. While we were there, I got a call requesting my presence in Montreal for the awards ceremony that had also seen a format change—the three finalists in each category were to appear, and then one would come away with the trophy. This was a big deal, during the playoffs and all. But if it was such a big deal, why hadn't I been informed more than two days before the ceremony? I was tired, I was on vacation, and besides, I was still annoyed from the previous year, when I had brought Jill to Toronto for the announcement only to discover that she wasn't allowed in the

Hot Stove Lounge at Maple Leaf Gardens. It was men only. Jill had to leave me when I went inside the building. She wished me luck, then went to visit my parents, who had since moved to Toronto.

Anyway, I never did catch a plane from Florida for Montreal, where the Canadiens were playing the Blues in the Stanley Cup Finals. Tommy Ivan, among others, tried to talk me into going, but I refused. While I was in Ft. Lauderdale, I found out that I had won three trophies again. I knew I would win the Art Ross for most points, but I also won a second straight Lady Byng, beating out Johnny Bucyk of Boston, and the Hart Trophy as most valuable, beating out Beliveau.

The league wasn't too happy about my no-show, and in retrospect, the league was right. I apologized to Mr. Campbell. I had my reasons for not making the trip, but sometimes you have to swallow hard and do what you're supposed to do. I took some grief for my stance, from fan mail to press clippings, and I deserved all of it. I was grateful for the awards, and I always felt privileged to be in the NHL. I'll never forget the NHL All-Star Game when I centered for

Bobby, whom I consider the greatest left wing in history, and Gordie, the greatest right wing in history. It was an exhibition, yet I was as nervous as I'd ever been. I just wanted to get out of the way of those two giants. But I was glad to be there, believe me, and I should have been at that ceremony instead of in Florida. It was my mistake, and I had to live with it.

We finished last in 1968–69, the second year of expansion, and a strange year to boot. We finished above .500 and we scored a bunch of goals—including 58 by Bobby—but we gave up a bunch too, and missed the playoffs. During the summer, Pit Martin blasted the organization for having no direction and operating with different rules for different players. I didn't make much of his remarks, although he did receive the nickname of "Perfect Pit," though not from me. More importantly, during the summer we got a goalie, Tony Esposito, from Montreal. Tommy Ivan let Phil go to Boston but he got Tony from the Canadiens, and for only $25,000, the waiver price. It was an absolute steal. Montreal couldn't use him, but we sure could and did. We also brought in a few other rookies, notably Keith Magnuson and Cliff Koroll.

The following season was amazing, right up until the last game. We had lost our first five games of the year and, after our last-place finish the year before, Chicago fans were restless. You started hearing the "Good-bye, Billy" chant in the Stadium. We were only a .500 team in early January, but then we went on a real tear and lost only seven games the rest of the way. Tony O was tremendous. As a rookie goalie, he collected 15 shutouts, which is still a modern record. He reminded me a lot of Glenn Hall, except that Tony didn't throw up before games. Instead, Tony got prepared by just sitting in front of his locker, without saying a word, staring off into space. You didn't dare talk to Tony before a game. His wife, Marilyn, didn't even try. He would just look through you like you were invisible.

Entering the final night of the season—April 5, 1970—we were tied with Boston for the top of the Eastern Division with 97 points. But we had five more victories, which was the tie-breaker, so if we beat Montreal at the

Stadium, it didn't matter what the Bruins did at home that night against Toronto. But there was another subplot. The Rangers had routed Detroit that afternoon to equal Montreal's 92 points in fourth place, so the Canadiens had to beat or tie us to reach 93, or score at least five goals, which was the next-tie-breaker with the Rangers. By the eighth minute of the third period, we were up 5–2 and the fans were going crazy. Boston was beating Toronto, but it didn't matter. "We're No. 1! We're No. 1" That's all you heard from a standing-room-only crowd. No more "Good-bye, Billy."

The Canadiens' coach, my old friend Claude Ruel, had to make a decision. He pulled his goalie, Rogie Vachon, for a sixth skater. Remember, the Canadiens still needed to score three more goals to qualify for the playoffs. Well, we wound up scoring five empty-net goals to whip Montreal 10–2 and clinch first. It was nuts. The Canadiens and Maple Leafs both missed the playoffs—a dark day for Canada—but we carried Billy off the ice after finishing first for only the second time in Blackhawks history. Unfortunately, after sweeping Detroit in the first round, we were eliminated from

the playoffs in four straight by the Bruins, who were starting to build a powerhouse.

The result was another postseason disappointment for us, but we were justifiably encouraged by the new blood on our roster. Koroll became my right winger, my roommate, and a close friend to this day. Magnuson was a piece of work. He went to the University of Denver, as did Koroll, and came into our training camp like his pants were on fire. Maggie was a redhead with a lot of spirit. We saw that right from our first exhibition game when he climbed the stairs from our locker room and hit the ice in full stride. Most guys skate rather easily at the start of practice or for a pregame warmup, but Maggie looked like he was in a race. A lot of times, you find that players with that attitude are doing it for effect. Not Maggie. He was the real thing.

He wound up making the team without ever spending a day in the minor leagues. He made the most of his talent, and he would fight anything that moved if he thought it would help the team. Maggie was a great guy off the ice, but—how can I say this politely?—he could be gullible on occasion. Crusty, cruel veterans like

Pat Stapleton and yours truly took advantage of this. We indoctrinated rookies in various ways, but Maggie was perfect for one of our favorite stunts, the snipe hunt. We convinced Maggie that the snipe was a bird and, as a team outing, we would all go on a snipe hunt one evening. He was full of enthusiasm, naturally.

And naturally, there is no such bird as a snipe. But before our big night, we had him practicing calls. "Here, snipe…here, snipe." We drove him out to a cornfield in Hillside, a Chicago suburb, although we told him we were in Wisconsin. Then we sent him out with this bag which he was supposed to use to collect the snipe once he caught them. We told him all of us would be in the cornfield when, in fact, we just left him out there alone with his bag and his lantern while the rest of us went to a nearby bar.

Of course, we alerted the local police, who were also in on the gag, as was Billy Reay. Before too long, the cops showed up and asked Maggie what he was doing. Why, I'm snipe hunting, Maggie said. Well, the cops replied, that's illegal without a snipe hunting license. The cops hauled him into the station and even set up a makeshift, make-believe courtroom. They put Maggie in a cell. He was sweating bullets. He thought he was going to jail. He even asked if he could contact Stan Mikita, not knowing that I was one of the ringleaders. They asked him how he knew who Stan Mikita was. Maggie said I was a member of the Blackhawks. The cops told him he was full of it.

Soon enough, the rest of us showed up at the station, trying not to laugh, and there was even a fake judge on hand. Stapleton stepped up and said, "What happens if Billy Reay finds out about this?" Maggie lost it. Turned completely white. He was petrified. Even us old guys couldn't keep a straight face for long, so just about when Keith thought he was headed for the slammer and his career was over, we let him in on our little joke. I could tell you that Maggie got wise to us after the snipe hunt, but that wouldn't be true. We continued to torment him. I can't count the number of times Stapleton convinced Maggie that he was about to be traded.

\\\\\\\\\\\

If there's a season that still haunts me, it would be 1971. We had a hell of a team. Bill White,

who came over to us in a great trade by Ivan the year we went from last to first, formed a top defensive tandem with Stapleton. Tony was terrific again, Bobby had 44 goals, brother Dennis scored 40, and we lost only 17 games, finishing first for a second straight year with 107 points. After sweeping Philadelphia in the opening round, we had a classic seven-game series that featured three overtime games against the Rangers, beating them 4–2 in the clincher to advance to the Finals against Montreal.

We won the first two games at home, lost two there, won Game 5 at home, lost Game 6 in the Forum, and then came back to the Stadium for Game 7—May 18, a warm Tuesday night. We took a 2–0 lead and Bobby Hull came *this* close to making it 3–0, except the puck hit the post beside their goalie, Ken Dryden. Right after that, Jacques Lemaire picked up a puck near the blue line, fired it on Tony, and the thing knuckled. Tony missed it, our lead was cut in half, and that turnaround really affected us. It was like our hearts were cut open. We lost 3–2 when Henri Richard scored in the third period. I try not to think about that game, but

I have to when people bring it up. Still hurts, 40 years later.

In 1972, after we got knocked out of the playoffs by the Rangers, the entire landscape of hockey changed. A rival league, the World Hockey Association, was starting up, and that spring, the big news hit us all between the eyes: Bobby Hull was jumping to the Winnipeg Jets after 15 years with the Blackhawks.

What a shock. My pal Koroll thinks that if we had won the Cup in 1971, we would have begun a run of several Cups and that Bobby never would have left. I don't know about that. Bobby made a financial decision. He had had his contract battles with the Blackhawks, and the WHA offered him a deal that was hard to turn down—in addition to his yearly salary of $250,000, he got a $1 million signing bonus after all the teams in the new league chipped in to steal a superstar.

No doubt Bobby put the WHA on the map. I remember hearing rumors about a rival

league, but I never paid much attention to them. Bobby and I never really talked seriously about him making a move either, although we heard rumors. By 1972, I had hired an agent from International Management Group in Cleveland and, after Bobby took off, my representative, Peter Kuhn, got a call from the WHA people. They wanted to talk to me, too. I listened. Jill says the WHA wined and dined me. If memory serves, I was offered $1.5 million over five years to play with Chicago's team in the new league, the Cougars. Their owners, Jordan and Walter Kaiser, might have figured it would make a big splash if they got me to leave the Blackhawks. Kuhn suggested that I think it over very carefully, and I did. That money was significantly more than I was making with the Blackhawks.

I had many things to consider, starting with my family. We were very happy in Chicago, a great city with great people. Money is nice, of course, but Jill and I didn't live extravagantly. We just wanted the kids to have decent clothes, eat good food, and get a good education. I also believed in loyalty. I know it sounds corny, but I had worn a Blackhawks jersey for so many years and the Wirtz family had been good to us. I

TONY ESPOSITO

Stan was tough as a player. People tend to forget that because he made everything look so easy and was such a prolific scorer, but he was tough. Really tough. He played more than 20 years, and in those days, the game was different. There was all kinds of rough stuff. Interference, obstruction, and if you slashed a guy, you could knock him out and might only get a two-minute penalty. It's not like that now. So to be Stan's size and play at such a high level, and for so long without a helmet, he had to be tough. Most guys Stan's size didn't last in the NHL back then, and you better believe other teams went after him.

Now, we all know Stan spent a lot of time in the box himself during the early part of his career. But he cleaned his game up because he realized he was a lot more valuable on the ice than he was sitting out for a penalty. He also probably realized he wasn't going to last too long being his size and being so chippy. You live by the sword, you die by the sword. Plus, he had so much talent, why waste it? He changed his style, but he never went soft. He just played smarter. More control, stayed on the ice more. Guys liked to run him, but he loved it when a defenseman came right at him because Stan would just dump the puck off to someone who was open. Stan was never that fast. He didn't have great speed. But he could maneuver with or without that puck.

Beyond all that, he was a great teammate. When I joined the Blackhawks as a rookie in 1969, the two superstars—Stan Mikita and Bobby Hull—were really good to me. I knew Bobby a little through my brother, Phil, who played in Chicago before he was traded to Boston. But I didn't know Stan or his wife, Jill. They were really nice to my wife, Marilyn, and me. Like I said, Stan was a superstar, but he was never loud or arrogant. He never acted like he was anything special. He was the same as he is now, just a regular guy. He just doesn't smoke anymore. I couldn't believe how many guys were into cigarettes when I joined the Blackhawks. Ashtrays in the dressing room! Stan used to puff away pretty good, even between periods.

I practiced against both Bobby and Stan, of course. Bobby was no fun to practice against with that shot of his, high and hard, although he took it easy on me. Stan, you could watch and see how smart he was. Stan could sense how a play might develop, and he was terrific at making plays. In games, Stan would never just shoot the puck to get a shot on net. With some guys, you look at the statistics after a game and it says they had 10 shots. Yeah, but how many were from 60 feet out? Stan waited until he was around the faceoff circles. That's where he was really dangerous. And he was very unselfish. A superstar, but just one of the guys. He was really well-liked and, of course, respected.

When I came to the Blackhawks, it was after a year when they finished last and there had been some grumbling among the players about how there were special rules for Bobby and Stan. As a result, according to the guys who complained, the team was too offensive-minded and not concerned enough about checking. My opinion was this: if you have a guy who scores 50 goals and another guy who scores 100 points, they don't have to worry about coming back in our zone to play defense. I'm the goalie. I'll take responsibility for making the saves, and let those guys who can score like mad do their thing.

Tony Esposito played for the Blackhawks from 1969 until 1984, registering 74 shutouts, the most in team history. He was inducted into the Hockey Hall of Fame in 1988 and his No. 35 has been retired by the Blackhawks, for whom he currently serves as a team ambassador.

suppose I could have used the WHA as leverage with the Blackhawks, but I don't believe in working that way. Besides, I do remember in casual conversations with the WHA and the Cougars that I mentioned the word *escrow*. I wasn't totally convinced a new league could make it, and if they did, for how long. Although I wasn't sure of a lot of things, I was pretty sure that Arthur Wirtz and the Blackhawks were not going to go broke. But when I asked if all that WHA money would be guaranteed, no matter what, I never really got an answer.

Meanwhile, Tommy Ivan suddenly contacted me about a new contract with the Blackhawks featuring a very, very nice raise. He did that with several of my teammates, including Dennis Hull, Jim Pappin, and Pit Martin. I signed a new deal, and like a lot of guys, I bowed in the direction of Winnipeg, thanking Bobby Hull for driving salaries up to levels they had never been before. Not only did guys who jumped earn money they never dreamed of making, so did a lot of guys who didn't jump. The WHA lasted seven years, and not only did players get rich, so did the lawyers. There were a lot of lawsuits filed, including one by the Blackhawks contesting the legality of

Hull's departure. It was a very turbulent time for hockey.

We went to the Stanley Cup Finals in 1973 despite the absence of Bobby, but were beaten by Montreal in six games. We fell upon some lean times after that. The WHA certainly changed the face of hockey. Some players who probably wouldn't have made it to the NHL got to play in the pros. Other stars jumped. Gordie Howe got to play with his sons in the new league. Meanwhile, after the Boston Bruins won two Stanley Cups, the Philadelphia Flyers won two in a row with their "Broad Street Bullies" style. Then Montreal ran off four straight Cups in the late 1970s. We were not really contending, and management tried a lot of maneuvers to help bring some of the fans back who had left the Stadium. Bill Wirtz, our president, brought Bobby Orr in from Boston as a free agent in 1976, but Bobby's knees were pretty much shot. He played just 26 games for the Blackhawks before he retired at age 30, which is sad. We made a huge trade with the Atlanta Flames for Tom Lysiak. And we also underwent a coaching change.

Just before Christmas in 1976, I got a call from Tommy Ivan. The team was struggling, and I was told there would be a meeting with Bill Wirtz. I had no idea what was going on. The team was on the road, but I wasn't with them because I was injured. I showed up to the Bismarck Hotel where I ran into Tommy and Michael Wirtz, Bill's brother. Also there were Orr and White. Both of them were also hurt. I looked at Bobby and asked him, in pantomime, what was going on He pointed to White. He was the new coach. Bobby and I were going to be his assistants. It was all very strange, and it got even weirder when we were in the meeting and heard that Mayor Richard Daley had just died. The Wirtzes and Tommy, just as Bobby had indicated, said they were going to appoint Bill White as head coach. Would Orr and I agree to be his assistants? I didn't know what to say. I was still an active player and wanted to continue playing when healthy. I had no real plan or desire to coach.

"I have no experience coaching, especially coaching my teammates," I said. But as it was explained to me, Bill would be the boss while Bobby and I would be by his side as assistants. If it meant that I would be a player/coach, so be it.

I don't know what would have happened had I told them no, but I said okay. Meanwhile, I was thinking about Billy Reay, who had been my coach since 1963. I had a terrific relationship with him, and I felt for him and his wife, Claire. Deep down, I really believed that if this group of players was not going to produce for Billy Reay, they weren't going to play for anybody. Long before the term "players' coach" became common, Billy was just that. He wasn't much for speeches or meetings or showmanship. He expected guys to be ready for games, play hard, and play to win. He never overcoached. He never had to tell you who was boss because everybody knew he was it. Only after this whole shakeup occurred was it revealed in newspaper stories that Billy got fired by a note under his office door at the Stadium. When White was asked what his first move would be as head coach, he responded, "I'm going to take all my doors off their hinges." Funny guy, that Bill White. At least the Blackhawks took good care of Billy Reay after he was dismissed. Bill Wirtz made a point of having him come to all the games, sitting right near our bench.

As for the tri-coaches system, it was a farce. I know I didn't like it, and I didn't have to deal

NO. 500

Stan Mikita scored the 500th goal of his National Hockey League career on February 27, 1977, at the Chicago Stadium, becoming at the time just the eighth player to reach that mark beside Gordie Howe, Bobby Hull, Phil Esposito, Maurice Richard, John Bucyk, Frank Mahovlich, and Jean Beliveau.

Mikita registered his historic goal at 13:56 of the third period against Cesare Maniago of the Vancouver Canucks, who defeated the Blackhawks 4–3 before about 12,500 fans. Mikita took a pass deep in his own end from defenseman Phil Russell, carried the puck the length of the ice, split the defense, and lifted one over the sprawling goalie.

"I haven't heard cheers like that since Bobby Hull left," quipped Mikita, who was surrounded by teammates who left the bench for a brief celebration. "It was a thrill and a relief. I'm real happy it came before the home fans. I've got to thank them and my linemates, Cliff Koroll and Dennis Hull, who were trying to set me up all night."

"Typical Mikita," said Orland Kurtenbach, Vancouver's coach. "He had guys hanging all over him, and he still scored."

—Bob Verdi

with it for long because the next season, the Blackhawks hired Pulford to be GM/coach. He had a very good run coaching the Kings after he retired, and he was going to do both jobs for us. Tommy Ivan was moved into a different office, and Pulford was put in charge. I wasn't getting any younger, of course, and I don't think I need to remind you that Pulford and I were not friendly at all from our playing days. I didn't sense that this would be the beginning of the end for Stan Mikita. I sensed that it was the middle of the end.

My instincts were correct. I was asked to attend the press conference announcing Pulford's arrival with the Blackhawks, but I was away at the time in Canada and didn't make it. He wanted as many players there as possible, and whether he was upset that I wasn't among them, I don't know. But my contract was up, and my first offer from him was for a 75 percent pay cut. I learned of that from my agent, whom I didn't talk to for three weeks because he said he was too embarrassed to call. I'll spare you all the details, but after more time passed, I wound up playing for my previous salary—no cut, no raise—on a contract that I did not sign until the last minute, and not without a phone call from

Bill Wirtz. The team president got involved, for which I thank him.

My last couple seasons with the Blackhawks were difficult. I was fighting the usual aches and pains, plus the feeling I had that I wasn't really wanted. At first, I was told that I would be taking regular shifts and skating a lot of minutes during exhibition games. I didn't quite understand that. Was I being tested? But when the games that mattered began, I didn't really feel like I was part of the mix. Look, I'm not naïve about how things go in professional sports. When regimes change and a player is getting older, situations arise that create personal issues and problems. In 1979–80, I played just 17 games, scored two goals, and that was it. Most retirements do not end happily, but I went out after 22 years with my head high. I was ready to leave, but I hoped it would be different. I was wrong. As a result of the way things went down, I thought I was probably done with the Blackhawks forever. Fortunately, I was wrong again.

"MOST RETIREMENTS DO NOT

END HAPPILY, BUT I WENT

OUT AFTER 22 YEARS

WITH MY HEAD HIGH."

—STAN MIKITA

BOB MURRAY

When I came up to the Blackhawks in 1975, one of the first people who took an interest in me was Stan Mikita, an icon in Chicago. I was just a kid trying to find my way around, and he had me over to his house for dinner with him and his wife, Jill. It was early in the year, and we sat around all night and just talked. Stan always came at things in a different way, more philosophical, I guess. He would tell you what to expect, what to get used to, how things might happen, on and off the ice. It was terrific advice for a young guy like me, something he really didn't have to do.

Stan really cared about people and the team. A lot of superstars might not have made time for a rookie, but he always did. In a game or at practice, if my pass wasn't quite on the tape, he would never give you that look or let you have it verbally. Stan was never like that. He would take you aside and offer suggestions. How to do this, how to shoot the puck, how to play angles. Every player goes into a slump, and when that happened, he would take time to talk to you. "Murph, what are the two things you do best?" Well, I thought I was pretty good at skating and moving the puck. "Okay," he would say, "then just go back to that. Don't try and do everything. Just simplify the game and do what you do best." Which was a great tip. When you struggle, you tend to try to do too much. But he would tell you, no, go the other way. Keep it basic. And of course, he was exactly right. That was how you come out of a slump.

In his own way, he was definitely a leader. Not by being a rah-rah guy. Just by taking making time for teammates. He was especially good with young players. I don't know that I ever heard Stan raise his voice when he was trying to get a point across, but he was always there for you, and again, always in a different way than other people. Quiet, almost intellectual. Most superstars can't relate to guys who aren't superstars. They can't teach what they do. Like Wayne Gretzky later on, Stan was always ahead of the play. When you thought Gretzky was going to do something, he had already done it. It was like he had that sixth sense. Stan was that way.

Stan's wife, Jill, was great, too. That night at dinner, she said, "The minute I saw you, I knew you would be a good player because of the way you moved that puck. I told Stan you would be with the Blackhawks for a long time." For a kid coming to a team that had a lot of veterans, that was very uplifting to me. I felt like I was part of the family. Special people, Stan and Jill. And Stan cared about you after you were done playing. He would ask me about what I was going to do when I retired. After he moved on, he went into the golf business, and I wound up working with him for six years at a nice course outside Chicago, Kemper Lakes, where he was into golf management and pushed me in that direction. Stan saw the big picture. He was about more than just the 60 minutes every game night. I can't say enough good things about him.

*Like Stan Mikita, **Bob Murray** played his entire NHL career with the Blackhawks—1,008 games, the most for any defenseman in franchise history and the fourth-most of any player. Murray is currently general manager of the Anaheim Ducks.*

O CANADA

I n 1972, I was privileged to be on Team Canada's roster for what turned out to be an epic eight-game series against Russia. Canada basically formed a "dream team" of NHL stars to play four games in Canada, then four in Moscow, before the regular NHL season was to begin. It would be difficult to describe how big the "Summit Series" was in Canada, where hockey is like a religion. For me, there was added emotion because the Russians had invaded my country, Czechoslovakia, in 1968.

The ability of the Russians also contributed to the drama of the series. We had no idea how good they were, and it was almost as though they deliberately lulled us into a sense of overconfidence during their practices. We watched them and they looked awful. Then in Game 1 in Montreal, we scored in the opening 30 seconds and upped our lead to 2–0 before you could blink. I didn't play that game and was sitting with Bobby Orr, who was hurt. When we went up 2–0, Bobby said to me, "Let's get a beer…it's over." Not quite. The Russians came back and whipped us 7–3, and all of Canada was shaken.

Harry Sinden, the Boston Bruins coach who was coaching Team Canada, put me in the lineup for Game 2 in Toronto and we won 4–1. We tied in Winnipeg 4–4, then lost in Vancouver where the fans let us have it. We were going to Russia down in the series, and we left a very unhappy nation of Canada behind us. If we didn't rally, fans would have made mincemeat out of us. We might have had to stay out of Canada for a while.

Fortunately, we did make a great comeback and won the series when Paul Henderson scored with 34 seconds left in Game 8. I didn't play any of the games in Moscow. Our team had twice as many players on the roster as you could suit up, and with Bobby Clarke and Phil Esposito at center, I wasn't complaining. As it turned out, our team in 1972

was voted "team of the century" in Canada. Game 8 was such a huge event that schools were let out so kids could watch the telecast.

The only request I ever made of Sinden was that he let me play in Prague, where Team Canada went to play the Czechs after the pressure-packed series against the Russians. Harry agreed and even let me leave Moscow early to I could be with my family. Jill and I wound up watching Game 8 on this little black-and-white TV in our hotel lobby. There was this big, well-dressed Russian guy in the area, and we made a bet with him. After Henderson scored, we took that guy to the cleaners. Champagne for everyone. Ten bottles. Plus, he paid for dinner.

The game in Prague was very emotional. My mother, Emilia, was there, as were my sister, Viera, and brother, George. It was a proud moment for them, I'm sure, and it certainly was for me. Even though I didn't play that much against the Russians, the Team Canada experience was one of the greatest I've ever had. And to cap it off with a game in Prague was unbelievable. To this day, the location of the puck Henderson won the series with is a mystery. My teammate with the Blackhawks, Pat Stapleton, who was great against the Russians, supposedly has it in his possession. But Pat says his defensive partner on Team Canada, Bill White, swooped into the net and kept it for himself. White insists that Stapleton has it. Those two guys, Stapleton and White, were beauties. But they could play.

The series was a real eye-opener. Not only for Canada, but the world. The Russians wore uniforms that looked like they were from the Salvation Army instead of the Red Army, and practiced as if they really didn't have a plan, but they could really play. We've seen that in subsequent years, given the number of players who have come over and made a mark in the NHL. But in 1972, we just weren't going to let them beat us, no matter what.

"When it's all said and done, it's not how many goals or assists or trophies you collected. It's about what you have done as a husband and a father and whether you've handled those roles the right way."

—STAN MIKITA

CHAPTER FIVE

ALL IN THE FAMILY

Without question, my greatest accomplishment in life was convincing a wonderful woman like Jill to become my wife, especially after she got over the fact that I wasn't Dollard St. Laurent.

Jill worked for Congressman Harold Collier of the 10th district of Illinois. In 1962, I was invited to attend a testimonial dinner for him. It happened to fall on the same evening as the annual dinner held by the Standbys, the Blackhawks' loyal and active fan club. The players always went to their bash, and I wasn't sure I could make both. Thank goodness I did.

Jill had a passing interest in hockey at the time. By that, I mean she might go to some games but I don't believe she followed the sport closely. She did notice that No. 19 for the Blackhawks in the early 1960s was St. Laurent, a defenseman who helped us win the Stanley Cup in 1961. Players didn't wear helmets in those days, nor did we have names on the backs of our jerseys. He was a dashing and debonair Frenchman who was quite handsome. In later years, Jill said he wasn't merely handsome; she said he was gorgeous. I, of course, was not dashing or debonair or French, and although I've been called a lot of things in my life, gorgeous is not among them.

Anyway, a mutual friend, Mickey Madigan, introduced me to Jill. Stan Mikita, this is Jill Cerny. Jill Cerny, this is Stan Mikita. Jill was obviously disappointed, because she thought the Blackhawk she was about to meet was going to look like Dollard St. Laurent.

"Hello. Now if you'll excuse me, I'm extremely busy," she said. Jill took off, I settled down to watch the floor show with Bobby Hull and his wife, and I really didn't think I'd ever see her again. When Jill returned to the table about three hours later and said she'd have a drink with me, I was pleasantly surprised. I was also taken by her beauty—dark brown hair, brown eyes—and her personality. She was exceptionally bright and witty. I loved her sense of humor. I loved everything about her at first sight. I decided this was the woman I wanted to marry. I don't think she was as taken by me, but I did stop by her office the next day and took her to breakfast. Between her frequent trips to Washington, D.C., with Congressman Collier, we had a few dates that summer. Then I went to Washington to visit her, and eventually I took her to St. Catharines to visit my parents.

Now, I'm going to share with you a slight disagreement Jill and I have had for many years. My recollection is that during our time in St. Catharines, we took a walk around town and Jill saw a marquise-cut diamond in Murray Walters' jewelry store. She said she liked it. At least, that's my version of the story. Jill says, to this day, that nothing of the kind ever occurred. Either way, after Jill went back to Washington, I went to the store and bought an engagement ring with that marquise-cut diamond. A few weeks later, I drove from St. Catharines to Washington and managed to collect not one but two speeding tickets. I had been out the night before with the guys, overslept, and was in a rush when I finally got in the car. I got nailed twice on the Pennsylvania Turnpike, then got lost when I reached Washington. I had no idea where I was or where she lived. All of a sudden, I came to a red light and looked over at a bus idling next to me. Jill was on the bus! She was going home. So I followed the bus.

That night, I attended another of those political dinners. It was a long night and it got longer when Jill went back to the apartment

142

she shared with three other girls. They were all there, along with Jill's mother, Margaret; Congressman Collier; and several girls from the office and their dates. Everybody was talking and relaxing but all I could think about was that ring in my pocket. Finally, about 3:00 in the morning, everybody cleared out, I reached in my pocket, and I asked her to marry me. Jill was quiet for a minute, then said, "Well, we'll get engaged." She liked the ring, which I think proves that she must have first liked it when she saw it in the window of the jewelry store.

But enough of that. We met on March 6, 1962, were engaged that June, and then got married on April 27, 1963, at St. Mary of Celle Church in Berwyn, Illinois. Naturally, because we didn't want to make things easy on ourselves, we scheduled the wedding during the Stanley Cup playoffs. Why we did that, I'm not exactly sure. But Jill, always thinking one step ahead, lined up a proxy for me during the rehearsals. There were only two rounds of playoffs back then, but we were still cutting it close. Jill said if the Blackhawks had advanced to Game 7 of the Finals, it would have been played on our wedding day.

As it turned out, we were knocked out in the first round by Detroit, so I had two weeks to prepare for tying the knot. But in theory, we could have been married while I was playing hockey and a stand-in husband for Jill was at the church. The substitute was her uncle Jimmy, not Dollard St. Laurent. Several of my teammates were in the wedding. Glenn Hall was my best man. Bobby Hull, Steve Seno, Mickey Madigan, and Mike Ditka were also in it. Ditka was a star with the Chicago Bears, whom he eventually coached to victory in Super Bowl XX. Ditka became a legend in Chicago, but before that we hung out a fair amount off the field and played some golf during our off-seasons. Mike could have been a hockey player if he hadn't been a Hall of Fame tight end in the making. A tough guy, a real beauty.

Marrying Jill meant marrying into a large family because she had a number of relatives in the Chicago area. That was great by me, because her dad, Chuck, became more of a friend than a father-in-law. Chuck was a Czech.

He came to the rink with me on occasion, we played golf, and we enjoyed a few beers together. Jill's mother, Margaret, was also a wonderful person and a terrific cook, I might add. Margaret was Irish, and we named our first child, Meg, after her. Meg's middle name, Anne, was for my mother in St. Catharines. Jill was the middle child of three in her family—she had an older brother and a younger sister. Several times a year, we would have huge get-togethers, including an annual Christmas party at our place. I enjoyed everything about my relationship with Jill's family, and having Jill by my side made life all the more rewarding. She attended the University of Illinois and studied physical education. She went to work for Congressman Collier and never did finish school, but she gets straight A's as a wife and as a mother, and it's not because life was always easy. Jill had some health issues in her late twenties and early thirties. She also had two miscarriages, one shortly after she was watching me on TV and thought I had taken a puck in the eyes in Pittsburgh. That was between Meg and Scott. She lost another baby after Scott and before Jane.

The responsibility of bringing children into the world and maintaining a solid family affected our social life, of course, but who cares? What's better than having kids and watching them grow into adults? As a single guy, I liked to have a few beers, as do most hockey players I know, at least during our era. But I gave up drinking more than 20 years ago and gave up smoking at least 30 years ago. They often went together. In buildings around the NHL now, in just about every office building anywhere, smoking is strictly forbidden. But in our day, there were plenty of ashtrays strewn around the locker room because we had a number of guys who lit up before and after games and even between periods. I used to go through about a pack a day, at least until I had a health scare back in the 1970s. I thought I was having a heart attack and went right into intensive care. It was a Sunday morning during the summer. I stayed there for five days, taking every test imaginable. The doctors found nothing wrong with me. After I was cleared, I was relieved. When I left the hospital, the first thing I thought about was having a smoke. Then I thought again. What's the sense? Do I really need this? I took a pass, and

I haven't had a cigarette since, nor have I missed them. For liquid refreshment, I have developed a taste for nonalcoholic beverages. Very tasty and not fattening, although I have never had a weight problem, knock on wood. Being around cigarette smoke doesn't bother me, but I try to stay away when I can. Not because I'm afraid of being tempted, but because I just don't like the smell anymore.

In addition to being incredibly well-grounded, Jill is a lot of fun. She likes to dance, a lot more than I like to dance. Luckily, at various hockey functions throughout the years, Jill found a more willing dance partner than yours truly in Brian O'Neill, a longtime NHL executive who now handles the league's alumni. Mush March was another of her guys on the dance floor. He started playing with the Blackhawks in 1928, so he was even older than I am. But he had rhythm. Jill also has never been afraid to voice her opinion. If she has something on her mind, she's very likely to let you know about it, which is a quality I really admire. I know that trait has been a positive influence around our children and me, and

I believe that candor has its place in other situations, too.

I remember Tommy Ivan and Billy Reay once thought it would be a fine idea to have the players stay at a local resort, the Wagon Wheel in Rockford, Illinois, before home playoff games. They figured we'd avoid distractions during the most critical time of the season and would be able to get our rest without children and wives and neighbors around. How could we prepare for a game if we had to go to the store for a quart of milk in the afternoon? I didn't especially agree with the policy, and I had company in Jill. So she "suggested" to the front office that there be an alternative. Why not let the guys stay at home alone during the playoffs, then send the wives and children to a nice resort? If you want the guys to be relaxed, why not have them sleep in their own beds instead of at a hotel? She also pointed out that the wives and families were good enough to be with their husbands for six months of the regular season. If it was too much commotion during the playoffs, then send the wives and kids away. I don't know if Jill ever really got an answer about that. Personally, I thought it was just fine hanging around the house on the afternoon of a playoff game. If I wanted a nap, which I usually did, I had no problem finding peace and quiet.

Jill has been very understanding about a few of my eccentricities. One of them, for a brief period in my life, was sleepwalking. We were at a dinner for Doug Mohns in Sudbury, Ontario, in 1967. In fact, it was the night that Phil Esposito found out he had been traded from the Blackhawks to Boston. Phil was there, and he took it hard. I went on one of my nocturnal excursions, and Jill had to get out of bed and find me. At our own house, I also did some crazy things. I might wake up in the middle of the night feeling an urge to have some ice cream. By the time I got from the bedroom to the kitchen, I would set off all the alarms. Apparently, I came back to bed with my dish of ice cream as though nothing had happened.

As a "hockey wife," Jill was outstanding. After we got married, she attended all the games, usually sitting with her mother and Nancy Maki, Chico's wife. Jill said that her mother got more

excited than she did about what was happening on the ice. Jill said she brought crossword puzzles to the games. But I'm pretty sure she was keeping a close eye on the action, or at least on me. Jill was sensitive to what was written in the newspapers. If the press was critical of the Blackhawks or me, she might say, "What do the writers know? They never played the game." She didn't ask a lot of questions, though, about what was going on with the team and so forth. As long as I didn't get hurt, she tried to stay away from hockey talk. In a team atmosphere, there's always a certain amount of gossip that goes on, but Jill didn't care for it any more than I did. If something bad happened around the house or to the kids when I was on the road, she kept it to herself. She was not one to pick up the phone at home and call me while I was on a trip. She was also very good around the other wives. When young players came to Chicago with their girlfriends or wives, Jill was always willing to help, if asked.

She has said on occasion that she wonders whether the players now have as much fun as we had. My feeling is that you can buy an awful lot of fun with the salaries that are being

147

paid now. Her point is one I can understand, though. We would have played for nothing, and almost did. But we were all very close, the players and wives and our children. And we've stayed friends for years and years. Today's sports are more structured, more about business, and I don't know if that gets in the way of relationships or not. I'm not buddies with any of today's players. When we went on the road, we all got together for a few beers and then dinner. It wasn't just two or three guys. It was everybody, and it didn't matter what your salary was or your status on the roster. Jill and the other wives were the same way.

\\\\\\\\\\\\\\\

I'm incredibly proud of our four children. Jill and I always had a rule: they had to work. You hear stories about how kids whose parents have their names in the newspaper or on TV might tend to grow up spoiled and with their hands out. That never happened in our house, and I have to give Jill the credit for that. Obviously, when I was playing hockey, I was on the road a lot, preoccupied with games and practices, winning and losing. I tried to do my best, but Jill did

a fabulous job of raising our children and instilling values in them. She claims that when the kids were young they hated her because she was strict. If they had a car, they were going to have to feed it themselves. Mom and Dad weren't paying for gas. I don't know about the kids hating Jill, but I do know they followed instructions, or else. They did whatever they had to while they were around the house to earn a few bucks, whether it was working at McDonald's or whatever. When it was time for college, we told them we would pay for their education. But as Jill said, we aren't taking care of the other stuff, like deodorant and hair spray. Jill believed that the kids would never learn responsibility if they were handed everything on a silver platter. If I was a "celebrity," our children did not live like they were in a "celebrity" household. Not with Jill establishing curfews. The fact that Dad got asked for his autograph meant nothing. I never informed them about the generous $500 raise I once got from the Blackhawks.

Meg, our oldest daughter, graduated from Wheelock College, a small school in Boston. She majored in special education, and later received her master's degree in early childhood

education from Boston College. For the past 23 years, she has taught an inclusion class of children from ages three to seven at the Early Learning Center West in Boston. Inclusion classes educate students on education plans and "typically" developing children together in the same classroom. Her current class has students with visual, physical, and developmental disabilities and children on the autism spectrum, as well as their typically developing counterparts.

Jill and I have sat in on her class a few times, and it's a real eye-opener. When we first visited, I just looked at Jill and said to her, "How long can Meg continue doing this?" I thought five years maximum. Jill and I both had tears in our eyes when we walked out of there. It was clear that Meg wanted to keep doing it. I spent a fair amount of my free time through the years with the Special Olympics, which has meant a lot to me. All our children got involved in that, and also the Hearing Impaired Hockey School. They helped pin the medals on kids or be a "hugger" after each competition, and Meg told us that is where she developed the urge and initiative

to pursue a career in education. She feels that regardless of a given disability, children are more like each other than they are different and that everyone deserves an excellent educational experience. I'm not sure I can take credit for it, but my involvement with the various groups through the years certainly seems to have been an influence. Meg has two children of her own, Emily and Erin. Emily graduated from Phillips Academy Andover and is currently a student at Trinity College in Hartford, Connecticut. Erin is currently a student at Phillips Academy Andover as well as the backup goalie on the varsity hockey team. As you can see, Meg's girls are scholars, just like their grandfather.

Our son Scott is two years younger than Meg. He is an actor. We had no idea he had that kind of talent when he was in school in Chicago, but for the last 10 years or so, he's been in New York performing in *The Phantom of the Opera*. That's a tough business, but he has never been out of a job. In the fourth grade, he sang in a school play. The day after, we got all these phone calls from friends and neighbors wondering where Scott got that magnificent

My son, Scott, and I at my Hockey Hall of Fame induction ceremony in 1983

voice of his. I know one place he didn't get it. If I sing in the shower, the water turns cold. Scott was in dozens of plays in high school, including *Bully*, a 150-minute production that was a one-man play. Then he majored in speech at Northwestern, a great university, and started plugging away at his profession.

Scott's role in *Phantom* is as a swing. That is, he knows most of the male roles, so if one of the actors is sick or is off for a night, Scott takes over. He might do multiple roles if more than one of the regulars is missing. That's a lot of lines to memorize, but he loves it and he's great. As a kid, if you asked him where he left something like his street shoes, he would have no idea. Now, he memorizes entire scripts. I tried to answer questions from reporters when I was playing in the best way possible, maybe even in a funny way. But those responses were spontaneous. I never memorized anything. Every once in a while, people would go to one of his shows and refer to me later as Scott Mikita's father. Like Meg, Scott was always busy. In the summers and during school, he worked in a butcher shop, a bakery, and then did his acting thing with various playhouses

and theater groups in the Chicago area. Scott was very humble. I don't think we realized what a great voice he had until we went to church one Christmas when he was young and heard him singing Christmas carols. I asked Jill where he got that voice, and she said, "God." Scott has two darling children, 10-year-old Hannah and eight-year-old Lily.

Jane and Christopher, our two youngest, live in the Chicago area where they work at our family business, Stan Mikita Enterprises. Jane earned a degree in fashion merchandising and design and a degree in business. She is married to Scott Gneiser, who caddies on the PGA Tour for David Toms. They have three children— Charlie, eight; Billy, six; and Tommy, five—all of whom are crazy about sports. They like to play everything and watch everything. When I was playing with the Blackhawks, it was not unusual for me to bring our kids down to practice every so often. They would just hang around the locker room and have a blast. A lot of my teammates had children and did the same thing. Now, it seems as though most of the players on the Blackhawks are kids themselves and are too young to have children of their own. When Scott and Jane bring the boys to the United Center for a game, they are glued to the action. I figured they would be good for 10 minutes, then get bored and want to go home and get something to eat. No way.

Jane and Scott's boys call us Stan and Jill. During the season and especially during the playoffs, Charlie will call our house early in the morning. Maybe about 7:00 or 7:15. He's already been on his computer and he knows all the scores and highlights from the night before. So, he gets me on the phone and fills me in. If it was a late game, I probably went to bed before it was over. But Charlie has all the headlines. He might also throw in a few editorial comments, such as, "Stan, did you see Alexander Ovechkin last night? I don't think he played very well." I can't honestly say whether they have a grasp on what I did, but I do get some questions from the boys once in a while. For instance, they might see a guy make a great play at the United Center or on TV. They'll ask me what I thought of the move. Then they'll follow it up with, "Stan, were you like that? Were you that good?" On occasion, when I'm at the United Center and they show a shot of the

My wife's parents, Chuck and Marge Cerny

ambassadors—Bobby, Tony Esposito, Denis Savard, and myself—on the big scoreboard, Scott and Jane's boys will look up and take it in. But they don't get too worked up over it. They're pretty low-key. Besides, they'd rather watch players who actually still play instead of guys who used to play.

To them, Stan isn't the guy who has his number retired or anything like that, which

is perfect. Stan is the guy who comes over to the house and plays catch in the street or putts golf balls in the backyard. Not long ago, Bobby Hull had a play date with the boys at their house. They had a great time, and sure enough, Charlie asked us a while later whether Bobby could come over again. Then Billy popped the next question: "Could Bobby have the hair that he had on when he was young?" Jane is a great mother and wife and also a great golfer. Six times, she won the women's club championship at our club, Medinah. One of them she won when she was eight months pregnant with Charlie.

Christopher, or Chris, is another of our college graduates. He went to Augustana College and got his degree in business. Jane handles most of the numbers for Stan Mikita Enterprises, but Chris has also done a great job for the company. He and his wife, Jennifer, have two girls: Kayla, 10, and Megan, six, which rounds out our gathering of nine grandchildren. We are fortunate to have some loyal, longtime clients and associates in our business, but that does not mean Chris takes them for granted. He is extremely good about staying in touch

with the people we do business with, meeting with them, and inquiring about their needs. He does not just sit on his behind.

All our children are doting parents, and I would like to think they believe in a loving family atmosphere because that's how they grew up. Needless to say, when we have a family get-together, it's a free-for-all. A nice free-for-all, mind you, but a free-for-all. All our kids and their kids know that our door is always open to them, and the grandchildren think nothing of deciding on their own that they'd like to have a sleepover at Jill and Stan's. Jill says she sees different mannerisms in our children that indicate how they absorbed some of the lessons they learned while growing up, not the least of which was the value of a strong work ethic. She says she marvels at how some of the things they didn't like about our rules are now applied, almost subconsciously, in their own households. Jill and I obviously care about our children's families, but we try to stay away from asking too many questions. If there's a problem, we're here to help. If any of our children call and ask to talk about something, Jill and I both will get on the phone to have a conversation.

155

Otherwise, we let them live their own lives. I can observe, though.

When it's all said and done, it's not how many goals or assists or trophies you collected. It's about what you have done as a husband and a father and whether you've handled those roles the right way. I'm thankful for being blessed with not one but two sets of great parents, and a gift to play a game that would provide for the people I love. But I was especially lucky to have met Jill. The stress of raising children when the father is on the road so often has to be extreme, not that I would know because she handled it so well. Meanwhile, we have met some wonderful people and shared a lot of good times as a couple along the way. When fans look at me as the star of the family, I beg to differ. If you have a great wife and a happy home, it makes it a whole lot easier to go out and play a game. If you can have a few chuckles along the way, that makes it even better.

Years ago, Jill and I were at a fund-raiser where we sat next to a minister and his wife.

One of the planned activities was playing the marriage game, during which couples were asked how they first met. The husband would write his recollection on a piece of paper and the wife would write hers without either consulting the other. The minister and his wife went ahead of us, and their versions matched perfectly. He was in the church and she was in the choir and they looked at each other and they knew they were made for each other. The audience clapped. Then it was our turn. I was perfectly content stating that Jill and I first met at a testimonial dinner for Harold Collier. Then it was Jill's turn to enlighten the audience: she said we first met in the back of a '57 Chevy. There might have been a thousand people in the ballroom, and they were all rolling in the aisles with laughter (except for the minister). But like I said, Jill has a great sense of humor.

After we got married, Jill and I recounted the Dollard St. Laurent story. She insists she wasn't disappointed. Only confused.

"By now, I thought for sure that I would be forgotten. Instead, I am still being remembered. How lucky can a guy be?"

—STAN MIKITA

HAPPILY EVER AFTER

Jill and I were spending the winter at our place in Florida when the phone rang in December of 2007. It was John McDonough, the new president of the Blackhawks. Bill Wirtz, the longtime team owner, had died in September. His oldest son, Rocky, took over the team and hired John in one of his first moves. John had been with the Chicago Cubs for years, the last few as their president. It was a bold move that created shockwaves in Chicago.

I knew John was a progressive and innovative executive, but I never imagined one of his innovative moves would involve me. As it turned out, he had some ideas about Bobby Hull and me. John was aware of how Bobby and I had left the Blackhawks in kind of a bad way and asked if I would be interested in becoming one of the team's ambassadors. In other words, would I like to become part of the organization again? Would I like to be part of the family again?

At first I thought it was a prank. Maybe one of my buddies had a few too many beers and decided it would be funny to pick up the phone. This call came out of the blue. What was I to think? Then John asked me if I had talked to Bobby lately, which I hadn't. John explained what he envisioned us doing,

"I don't know what to say," I said. He told me to think about it and call him back.

I hung up and looked at Jill. I asked her to pinch me. Was this really happening? I'd been waiting 30 years for this phone call, and now it had finally come. I had never held a grudge against the Blackhawks, I just felt that I wasn't wanted around the team or around the building. When I retired in 1980, the Blackhawks offered me two tickets to every game for the rest of my life. (I told them that instead of doing something for me, they should do something for other former players. More about that later.) But other than that and the night my sweater was retired in 1983, I didn't have anything to do with the team.

Shortly after I talked to John, Bobby called. He asked me what I thought of this amazing development. I told him that I was pleasantly surprised, to put it mildly. I subsequently learned that Bobby had some meetings with Rocky and John about past issues. I had no such problems except for that 30-year gap, so I called John the next day and accepted his offer. It was a classy gesture by the organization, and

I have to say that just about everything the Blackhawks have done under Rocky and John has been first class. One of the first statements John made when he took over was that the Blackhawks were "out of the grudge" business. He said that if the franchise wasn't at peace with its past, it could not properly look to the future. Without naming names, John was saying what we all knew. The Blackhawks did not have a good relationship with a lot of former players, and that situation was no secret to the fans, thousands of whom had also become alienated from the organization. When players left the Blackhawks, it was too often with bad feelings. Eventually, a lot of fans left the Blackhawks too, and it was Rocky and John's mission to bring them back.

In March of 2008, Bobby and I were introduced as ambassadors at the United Center. A couple weeks later, Tony Esposito, our Hall of Fame goalkeeper who also departed the organization under difficult circumstances, was announced as a third ambassador. Denis Savard became a fourth later that year. If you were to ask me for our job description,

I would say we do whatever we are asked to do. No job too small, no job too big. We help with marketing, promotions, special events, sponsors, you name it. The Blackhawks treat us and our families like royalty, but that seems to be the mission of the entire front office, which has developed a fan-friendly attitude. Rocky almost immediately directed that home games be put on television, an idea that his father vehemently opposed. John beefed up his staff with young and energetic people, and the turnaround was staggering.

It did not hurt that the product on the ice was improving.

By being down for so long, the Blackhawks had acquired high draft choices, and they used them wisely to select kids like Jonathan Toews and Patrick Kane. But just as importantly, the franchise came out of the dark ages off the ice. John said that the Blackhawks had lost an entire generation of fans, maybe more. I can't argue with that. There were thousands of empty seats in the Chicago Stadium after the team's last trip to the Stanley Cup Finals in 1992, and there were even more empty seats in the huge United Center after it opened in 1995. But fans aren't stupid. They know when an organization is solid, and they returned in droves. Chicago is a great hockey city, but the fans had fallen out of love with the Blackhawks. When John declared that his goal was to win the Stanley Cup, he meant it, and the fans believed him. Lo and behold, the goal was realized only three years after Rocky and John assumed control. The Blackhawks won their first Stanley Cup since 1961 in 2010, beating the Philadelphia Flyers in six thrilling games.

Rocky became a folk hero in Chicago. He spent money to make money, reached out to the fans, and even sat among them during games. The Blackhawks provided a suite for the ambassadors to watch home games from, but Rocky sat in the stands. Whatever he and John did seemed to work. It was as though they wrote the book on how to revive a franchise that had been dormant for too many years. Naturally, tagging along for the ride was thrilling. Not only did I feel wanted again, but it was a blast to be part of this great organization. People in Chicago were talking hockey again. Tickets were scarce. And at the Stanley Cup parade, police estimated 2 million people showed up in the Loop to celebrate. I was on one of the last double-decker busses with my fellow ambassadors, and if you looked down the side streets, you would have thought some of those people were going to wind up in Lake Michigan. The crowds were that thick. People were hanging out of the windows. Crazy. Judging by that parade, the huge TV ratings, and the perpetual sellouts in the United Center, I'd say hockey is back where it belongs in Chicago and back where it used to be.

One personal note. When John talked about a lost generation, it made complete sense to me. Still, I was completely surprised by the number of young people who showed up at the United Center to watch the "new" Blackhawks. Many of them were so young that they came with parents who remembered the good old days. But what really caught my attention was how all these young people seemed to have a sense of history. John said he wanted to

connect the dots, and those parents probably helped. But I had kids coming up to me or applauding when my mug was shown on the scoreboard at the United Center who could not have possibly watched me play. Or Bobby. Or Tony. If they saw clips of us playing, the clips had to be in black and white. Yet, even among that "lost generation," there was an idea about how the Blackhawks used to be. Before Toews and Kane, maybe there was Hull and Mikita. I never, ever expected that kind of atmosphere. The 2010 Blackhawks were current events and the best team in hockey. But somehow, all those fans, many of them new to the game, had an appreciation for what came before. Perhaps that occurred because Rocky and John were the same way. They were building a modern organization, one that became the envy of the NHL almost overnight, yet they too understood who came before them. A lot of us old guys put in a lot of sweat for the Blackhawks, and it was nice to be appreciated. Meanwhile, by the end of the 2010–11 season, there had been 146 consecutive sellouts at the United Center, where the season ticket base went from 3,400

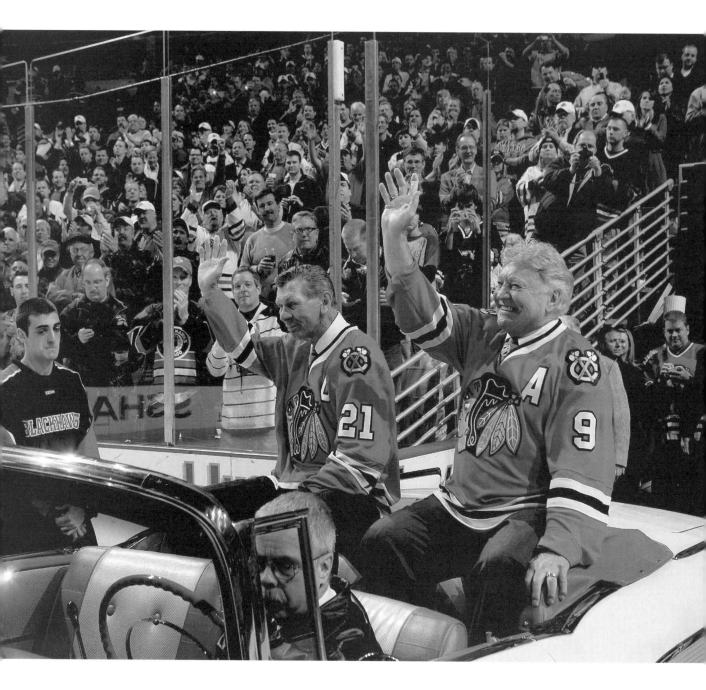

to more than 14,000 under the new regime. Impressive.

As players, Bobby and I used to make some appearances around Chicago, mostly on Mondays when we were usually off. For that, the Blackhawks would pay us $25 each. It was a good way to make a few extra bucks and also meet the public. Maybe that helped people from past generations remember us. But what the Blackhawks under Rocky and John and Jay Blunk do now as far as marketing the product is on a completely different level. When John and Jay were with the Cubs, they helped Wrigley Field become a destination point. They promoted the ballpark and the team tirelessly. In the old days, NHL teams didn't do much of that. Management figured that you opened the doors on game nights and the rinks would fill up, which they usually did. But the new Blackhawks come up with different ways to sell hockey in Chicago, even when there are no seats available. When the team won the Cup in 2010, McDonough celebrated for a little while, then said, "The party's over." He was planning for the next year as soon as the parade ended. Why?

Because he wants to build an organization that competes every season. He thinks long-term, which is one reason he's been so successful. It would be easy, after you've won a Cup and your season ticket waiting list is huge, to rest on your laurels. Not Rocky, or John, or Jay.

On top of everything the Blackhawks did for us old guys, they held this unbelievable event to open the 2009–10 home season. They began their season in Finland, another indication of how the NHL in general and Blackhawks in particular have expanded their horizons. What once was a six-team league was now a league of 30 franchises, playing a little bit abroad and even outdoors! The league's Winter Classic on New Year's Day has become a ratings bonanza, and not surprisingly, the Blackhawks under John McDonough landed one for Wrigley Field on January 1, 2009, against the Detroit Red Wings. The place was packed and national interest was through the roof.

What the Blackhawks did on October 10, 2009, had a more local flavor. Shortly before they were to begin their home opener against Colorado, I got a call. McDonough wanted all four of us ambassadors to skate onto the ice before the game. I hadn't been skating too much, but I was game. So were Bobby, Tony, and Denis. I checked my old blades that had been hiding in the garage, and we went to the United Center for a practice the day before the game. It's one thing to be honored on the ice; it's another to be honored while you're *skating* on the ice. How management kept this idea a secret is amazing, but nobody seemed to know about it. When the time came, we skated out one by one from the west end of the United Center, near where the Zamboni enters. It was quite an event. I came out third, behind Denis and Tony, and we were all there waiting for Bobby, who got up a little head of steam but might not have been able to stop if he hadn't have been intercepted by Jonathan Toews and myself. Bobby said later that if we hadn't grabbed him he might have gone right through the end boards.

The reception was fabulous. Again, I have no idea why we are remembered so fondly after all those years. But it was terrific. I can't speak for myself, but I will say this about Bobby. He spent hours and hours signing autographs for fans during his time with the Blackhawks. I did my share, but I wasn't in his league. Maybe some of those fans who got autographs 40 years ago told their children, who in turn told their children.

In that respect, the crowds at the United Center were a reflection of the new Blackhawks. For all their business savvy, Rocky and John believe in creating a family atmosphere. It isn't like the players stand over here, and everybody else is over there. The new management also has launched an annual summer convention where fans gather in a downtown hotel one weekend in July to salute the team and the game of hockey. John did it with the Cubs, and now the Blackhawks' convention is always sold out. When players are brought in to meet and greet fans, they don't come alone. It's the players and their families. Glenn Hall came in from his home in Alberta and he couldn't believe how well he was treated. "Sthahan," he said with that lisp of his, "this isn't like the old days. They make us feel like kings."

Not only are the Blackhawks different, the game is different. If you ever happen to see some of those black-and-white films from the 1960s, you'll notice that the game seems much slower than it is today. It's not an illusion. The NHL has more speed than ever, but also more size. The players are bigger, stronger, yet somehow faster. With the rules that were adapted after the lockout that wiped out the entire 2004–05 season, a lot of the old tactics are gone. Interference is a penalty. You can't hold and grab like you used to, even if you manage to catch some of these speedsters. As a result, the game is more wide-open. Offensively, I probably would have liked to play in my prime under these conditions because there's more room to roam. I liked the puck-possession style, and if a guy isn't giving you a two-hander on your ankles, you have a better chance of making a play. Then again, when I was doing stupid things on the ice, I got my share of whistles. If I acted like that under today's rules, I might spend an entire game in the penalty box. In all, I like what I see of the current product. On most nights, you'll be entertained. And if the game is tied after 60

minutes, they play overtime or have a shootout until it isn't tied anymore. Every game yields a result.

With all the size, however, there is still a place for a smaller guy. I ran into Martin St. Louis, a terrific player with the Tampa Bay Lightning, in the United Center in 2010. Even with his skates on, I was taller than him. But he's a star. Now the NHL is drawing players from all over the world. They train better and eat better than players from our era did, when almost all our players were Canadians. Obviously, the money now is on another planet from where we were. You have guys making $10 million a year. I can't knock it, though. God bless them. There's a hard salary cap, but I'm all for the players.

When I say I waited 30 years for that phone call from the Blackhawks, it's not that much of a stretch. I retired as a player in 1980, and they held a party of sorts for me in the Governors Room of the Stadium. It was a very nice gesture. A lot of people were there, and it marked my "official" start to another life, a life after playing games, real life. The timing was right. In 1979–80, I was able to play only

17 games and scored only two goals. My body, particularly my back, kept saying no. Time to go, Stanley. The Blackhawks had been in the playoffs in the four previous years but were eliminated in the first round each time without even winning a game. They broke that streak in 1980 but I was unable to play. I hadn't played since late November of 1979, in fact, a game in Vancouver where I was really hurting and knew it was about over for me.

Fortunately, I had established some groundwork for what I would do with myself after my playing career ended, and my immediate plans involved golf. I had the good fortune to become acquainted with Jim Kemper Jr. of Kemper Insurance, and his company had built a terrific golf course in Long Grove, Illinois, called Kemper Lakes. It would be the site of the 1989 PGA Championship, one of four majors on the men's professional golf tour, along with numerous other high-profile tournaments. He and Steve Lesnick, Mr. Kemper's right-hand man, encouraged me to look into a golf career, which I did. Even before I retired, I was hanging around Kemper Lakes, following around Bob

Spence, the head pro and director of golf, like a little puppy. Spence was a Southern gentleman who was great to me.

Spence did a fair amount of traveling on behalf of Kemper Sports Management, and when he wasn't around, I tried to learn the ropes. I always had enjoyed golf, so I dove into the golf business as best I could. Fortunately, I didn't need the money, but I did want to do something to keep busy and something that I enjoyed. We also had four kids to put through college, so a little extra income was nice. In order to become a Class A professional, I had to take certain written tests in addition to proving that I could play. I was decent enough at that. After all, if you want to become a teaching pro, you have to have some ability. I was probably a 2 handicap, which is pretty good. But you also have to go to school, to learn more about the business and rules and so forth.

When I finally got my Class A card, I started teaching, and my experience of being around Spence was invaluable. He really knew how to get his point across to his students, and I tried to follow his lead. I enjoyed trying to help people

with their game, and to see them improve to varying degrees was rewarding. Golf is a very difficult sport, and when you help a person who isn't very accomplished to see even the slightest sign of progress, it's satisfying to both teacher and pupil. I had the winters off too, which was nice, and I can't say enough for Mr. Kemper and Bob Spence. I have a lot of fond memories of my six years at Kemper Lakes.

I also had bought a couple of condominiums in Palm Harbor, Florida, as an investment. I was on an "allowance" of sorts from IMG, which helped keep me financially sound. IMG made some investments for me, and they worked out nicely. IMG was, and still is, a huge outfit. At the time, IMG represented most of the top tennis players. I was the first hockey player to join. In fact, I think I was the first athlete from a team sport to sign with them. In recent years, IMG has branched out into a lot of other fields, including representation of pro golfers. I was with IMG for a long time, maybe 25 years.

Meanwhile, I also went into business with Glen Skov, a former teammate of mine with the Blackhawks. We were involved in plastics,

a subject I knew nothing about. But Glen did, and he convinced me that my years as a pro hockey player wouldn't hurt as far as opening a few doors. So, we formed Mikita-Skov, and we did okay.

After a while, Glen decided he'd had enough of working, so I bought him out after 17 years and we set up Stan Mikita Enterprises, which still exists today. We are in the plastics and paper business, and our two youngest children—Jane and Chris—basically run the place. And they run it well. We have some great customers, notably Sal Ferrara of Ferrara Pan Candy and the Mullins family that supplies the sauces for McDonald's. We provide the packaging for those rather large firms. You have to put candy and sauce into some sort of container, right? Sal told me a story that relates to this idea of opening doors. He told me he was a stickboy for the Blackhawks years ago. I didn't remember him, but he reminded me that when I was a player, I went over to him one day. He said he was shaking because he thought he had done something wrong. I asked him at the time whether he had a girlfriend. He said yes, still shaking. Apparently, I reached into my pocket and gave him two tickets to one of our games. He said he never forgot that. It stuck with him, and he promised himself that if he could ever do something for me, he would. Well, we appreciate his business, believe me. And best of all, Sal has been a friend of ours ever since.

I don't know what I did to deserve loyalty like that.

I met Jack Mullins, the late owner of Mullins Food Products, at the Midwest Country Club in Oak Brook, Illinois. Jacked loved to play golf and when he could he joined Butterfield Country Club, a private club also located in Oak Brook. BCC hosts perhaps the finest tournament in the world, The Invitational, and I was once asked to fill in after another player became ill. That was my introduction to BCC, and until 2011 I played in that tournament for 34 years. Jack's son, Mike, is the oldest of 11 children and has been my tournament partner for 10 years. He also happened to be my caddy

in my first BCC tournament. He's an excellent player, a so-so caddy, and a great friend.

Jill, when she's in a mood to praise me, says that I never forget where I came from and that's why I never treated anybody like I was special just because I was a hockey player and they weren't. I will say that I never thought of myself as a star. When Jill had health problems, I did whatever I could to help out around the house. I cooked for the kids, I washed floors, I still cut my own grass. I don't remember what I cooked. Probably hot dogs. I also want to stress that Jane and Chris are not just sitting around, living off the family name. That's the way I was brought up, and that's the way they were brought up. Besides, they had better work hard at our business because I am the owner and the chief consultant.

※※※※※

I had other chances to be productive after retiring from hockey. Another friend offered me a car dealership. I knew even less about cars than I knew about plastics. That never materialized, luckily for the guy who made the

171

"I HAVE BEEN INCREDIBLY BLESSED.

I PLAYED A GAME I LOVE

AND I WAS ABLE

TO PROVIDE FOR MY FAMILY."

—STAN MIKITA

offer. But I was always dabbling in different stuff. While I was still playing and after I started wearing a helmet full time, I designed my own headgear. The first helmets used by hockey players were pretty cumbersome. Some guys thought they were too hot, others thought they were too heavy. I created one that was sturdy but lightweight. I made a little money off that, and sold the rights to a company that has since gone belly-up.

Another very important part of my off-ice life, when I was playing and then well after I retired, involved my friend Irv Tiahnybik. He was my personal critic who evaluated my performance when Ab McDonald and I got together for our lunches. One day in 1974, Irv approached me and asked me what I was doing during the second week of June. I said I would probably be playing golf. He said, no, we're going to start a hockey school for hearing-impaired kids. Irv had a son, Lex, who was crazy about hockey. He was a goalie, and he was also deaf. Irv knew that there were other youngsters in the same position, but they had nowhere to play. So, Irv was going to open a school for them. It would be called the Stan

Mikita School for Hearing Impaired, it would run for one week in the summer, and it would mean everything to these youngsters. We held it at a rink in Northbrook, a northern suburb of Chicago, and it really caught on.

We would bring these kids together from all over Chicago and the United States for practice sessions on the ice. Then, on Saturday night, we held a game featuring the hearing-impaired youngsters against the "Stan Mikita All-Stars," which was comprised of my old teammates. Our guys really went all out. They not only played in that game but contributed their time as guest instructors. That's one thing about hockey players and one reason I was proud to be one. Our guys on the Blackhawks wanted to relax during the summers, but I never had to pull any teeth to get guys to volunteer. Every spring they would ask me, when is the school? When can I be there? How much do you need me? It was a joy for us, and the kids were thrilled.

Irv and I were lucky to have a lot of friends who became involved, financially and otherwise, to help a great cause. I think I had an immediate understanding of what these kids

174

were experiencing. When I came to Canada from Czechoslovakia, I couldn't grasp what other people around me were saying because I didn't know the language. I might as well have been deaf. So I had a feel for what these kids were dealing with, including a lack of confidence and self-esteem. These kids loved hockey and wanted to find a place in the sport, but because they were hearing impaired, they encountered barriers.

What we wanted to do was teach them the game and the value of teamwork. That's what life is about. They had a sense of belonging at the school. It was a big deal for them, to play against their own and know that they were not alone. If they didn't understand what we teachers were trying to get across, we would use our hands to show them. At the end of the school, we would write a letter to their schools. If there was a hockey team at their high school or in their community, we wanted the coach to know that these young men had attended our school for one week and it would be nice if they could compete for a spot on the roster of a team where they lived. A lot of adults coaching youth programs want to win, of course, so

there was some trepidation about having a hearing-impaired kid on the team. Well, to make a long story short, Lex wound up making his high school team. He wore his hearing aid on his chest underneath all his equipment, and he played in a regular season game for his high school. I was on the road at the time, but Irv called me one night. Guess what happened? Lex played and his team won! Eventually, the team from our school won the gold medal at the Olympics for the hearing impaired, which was another giant step forward. They had something to reach for and they made it, just like Jim Kyte, a hearing-impaired defenseman who played for the Winnipeg Jets. When he found out about our school, he was there in a minute to help out. Then he opened a school of his own in Canada.

〰〰〰〰

I was also lucky enough to get in on the ground floor of another terrific organization, the Blackhawks Alumni. Jack Fitzsimmons, a great friend of the players, and Keith Magnuson were at the forefront of it. A few NHL franchises had alumni associations, and in the mid-1980s

175

Fitzie and Maggie brought up the idea of the Blackhawks starting one. I was all for it, and so was Bill Wirtz, the president of the team. Billy took some heat for a few of his ways as far as operating the franchise, but there was a side to him that most people didn't see. Bill loved Maggie. We all loved Maggie, who even coached the Blackhawks for a while. Bill was instrumental in helping us launch the Blackhawks Alumni by contributing not only some early money but also by providing a place where we could watch games together, first at the Stadium, then at the United Center.

But our association wasn't about just having a place to drink beer, tell old stories about how great we were, and establish connections for broken-down players in retirement. We established a scholarship fund, and our biggest fund-raiser was our annual golf tournament. The guys put my name on it. Why, I don't know, but I do know that the tournament has grown, as has the organization. Fitzie is gone and Maggie was killed in a tragic auto accident. Cliff Koroll, Maggie's best friend and my old roommate and linemate, is now president. In 1987, our first

scholarship check was for $1,000. Now, the we award three annually—to honor Maggie's old jersey No. 3—at $5,000 each for four years. To date, 78 hockey players from Illinois, male and female, have been given scholarships to college from the Alumni. Again, another reason I'm proud to have been a hockey player.

As for Maggie's death, I am still in shock over it. When I was playing, Kenny Wharram had to retire prematurely because of a heart ailment. He was still in his prime, he had just signed a new contract, and he was ready to go in training camp of 1968. But he had inflammation around the heart, and thank goodness, he caught it in time and is still with us. Jill and I were in Florida when we got the phone call about Maggie. It was December of 2003. Peter Marsh phoned in the middle of the morning and told me Keith had been in a car accident in Canada. Then Cliff called, bawling. It was terrible. Maggie was such a prince. I was crushed. We came back from Florida to attend the funeral. I'll never forget the line around the funeral home, thousands of people waiting in freezing weather to pay their respects. Then at

176

the church, Keith's son, Kevin, talked about how Christmas was always his dad's favorite time of the year. Then Kevin spoke about Keith's first Christmas in heaven.

Maggie was special. He touched a lot of people.

Shortly after I retired from the Blackhawks, there was talk of me maybe becoming an analyst on the broadcasts. I don't know whether I would have been any good at that, but I know it would have involved more traveling. I had had enough of that. As I told Jill, when I'm retired from hockey, we can go anywhere she wants, whenever she wants, and we won't have to be tied down by games and practices. Naturally, as she often reminds me now, I don't really feel like going anywhere, even for pleasure.

Another possible career move involved the Chicago Wolves, the minor league team in town. At one time, they had interest in me as some sort of front office type, maybe even as their general manager. That didn't pan out

either, and I can't honestly say I was too excited about the idea. I'm not cut out for sitting at a desk and doing paperwork on contracts. I also don't like the concept of living and dying with winning or losing. I did that as a player. I didn't need to do that in a suit and tie.

I did have a brief fling as an actor. Some of you might be old enough to remember the *Wayne's World* movies starring Mike Myers and Dana Carvey. There were two of them in the early 1990s that were based on their popular *Saturday Night Live* sketch. I went to Los Angeles for a couple of scenes where I played the proprietor of Stan Mikita's Donut Shop. It was actually more of a diner, and I didn't have much of a speaking part. I also got involved in those TV shows where athletes from a variety of sports try different skills, like swimming and running. I didn't come away with any trophies. But I did finish high school after I retired. At Jill's urging, I went to classes and got my equivalency diploma. I took a couple business courses and I graduated, better late than never. I completed my senior year when I was a senior citizen. Perfect.

177

DENIS SAVARD

When I joined the Blackhawks in 1980, Stan was just retiring. I wish it was like it is now in those days, because after Stan was done playing, we didn't see him around the Stadium very much. He said he didn't feel welcome, and we've all heard the reasons why. The whole thing was very unfortunate, but since he became an ambassador under the new management, Stan is around a lot, which is the way it should be.

Stan had to retire because of his back problems, and that kind of opened the door for me. I wish I had gotten a chance to play with him. When he was here for a brief time before he disappeared, he would jump on the ice once in a while and help kids like me, especially on faceoffs. As a center, of course, I was interested in everything he had to say. He was one of the best faceoff men ever, and gave me great advice. He talked about cutting that faceoff circle in half, and to make sure you have your half covered. The more you can go into the other half of the circle, depending on what the officials allowed you, the better. He also taught me that faceoffs are not just about technique. Faceoffs are about your will. It's you against the other guy, and the puck will be dropped differently and it will take a funny bounce here and there, but the big question is how much do you want it? Do you want the puck more than the guy you are up against? That was very valuable advice.

There is only one Stan Mikita, and to be just behind him in points in the history of this franchise, that is quite an honor. He was on the small side, just like I was. He told me, "They're out there to get you." He went through that as a player against bigger guys, and so did I. When I was trying to make it in the NHL, I heard that I was too small. He heard the same thing when he was young, I'm sure, and look at what a career he had. And I had a guy like Al Secord on my line to protect me. I'm not sure Stan had that kind of help. But he was so talented, he created room and made great plays anyway.

I watched him growing up. I had a cousin, Jean, who played briefly for the Blackhawks before I came up. I was 14, working at a restaurant in Verdun, where I grew up. It was owned by my uncle, and my dad was the manager. I was a busboy, and one night when the Blackhawks were in Montreal for a game, Jean invited the whole team for dinner. They all came and ate in a room upstairs. And there was Stan Mikita, right in the middle of the group. One table, all the way across, and Stan was right at the center. I didn't spend too much time picking up plates that night. I was in awe. I didn't want that night to end. Jean had told me stories about Stan, how he was a prankster, especially with the rookies. But the way Stan did things, he always made young guys feel comfortable. Stan was an icon who didn't carry himself like an icon.

Denis Savard registered 1,096 points with the Blackhawks, the third-most in franchise history behind Mikita and Bobby Hull. Savard was inducted into the Hockey Hall of Fame in 2000, and his No. 18 has been retired by the Blackhawks, for whom he currently serves as an ambassador.

In 1999, I had a brain aneurism. It came as a shock because I had had none of the usual symptoms that you associate with such a thing, like headaches. But I did have this persistent itch in my left arm. I wound up seeing a doctor and getting an MRI. The first one showed nothing, but then I went back for another that was more intense. I was on the table for three hours, and that's when they found trouble. If that balloon-like thing in your brain bursts, it's all over. My father in Czechoslovakia died of a cerebral hemorrhage. Dr. Robert Beatty, a neurosurgeon and family friend, told me I needed an operation and asked when I wanted to go under the knife. I told him I was planning to play in a golf tournament. Jill heard that and said, "If you drop dead, don't call!" I decided to have surgery right away, and it's a good thing I did. Dr. Beatty said I was close to the danger point. Four holes were drilled into my scalp. You can still see the scars. The itch went away.

I was lucky, but I bring this up because of the increased awareness in all sports about the dangers of concussions. As a player, I took a lot of blows to my head. We all did. But in our day, it was common to refer to the process as "having your bell rung." Well, as we've seen lately in some tragic cases of professional athletes, those shots to the head can result in brain damage that often isn't detected or doesn't manifest itself until well after players retire. The NHL and its alumni have been proactive about this problem. Other sports, like the National Football League, have followed suit. This is a serious issue, and I am willing to be part of a test group. While I'm alive, I will gladly cooperate with the investigation of post-concussion syndrome. It's the least I can do. And, without sounding too grisly here, if I can help after I'm gone, I will do that, too. Dave Duerson, a star with the Chicago Bears, recently killed himself because he realized he wasn't in full control of his senses anymore. In his suicide note, he specified that his brain be donated to the scientific study of concussions. It's a terrible story, yet a noble gesture by a man I knew.

I have been incredibly blessed. I played a game I love and I was able to provide for my family. I worked hard to be the best I could be, and I was not naïve enough to think that playing hockey allowed me other privileges. I received an honorary degree from Brock University in St. Catharines because of what I did on the ice. When Czechoslovakia was invaded by the Soviet Union in 1968, my mother Emelia and sister Viera were visiting North America. I got their visas extended through connections I had made from hockey. Because I was able to shoot a puck, I was put in several positions where I could help raise funds for charitable causes. And after being brought back to the Blackhawks, I have been able to share the joy of their revival while making a number of appearances that were fun, like singing "Take Me Out to the Ballgame" with my fellow ambassadors during the seventh-inning stretch of a Cubs game at Wrigley Field. Thanks to hockey, my family and I have met some unbelievable people and forged some lasting friendships. And the blessings keep on coming.

The Blackhawks are scheduled to open their 2011–12 season with another ceremony. Statues of Bobby Hull and I are to be placed outside the United Center. I don't know what to say. By now, I thought for sure that I would be forgotten. Instead, I am still being remembered. How lucky can a guy be?

On October 19, 1980, Stan Mikita's No. 21 jersey was retired, a first in franchise history, before the Blackhawks' game against the Washington Capitals at the Chicago Stadium. The banner was raised to the rafters behind the west goal with the years 1959–1980 on it, marking the career of the iconic center who never played a game in the minor leagues or with any other National Hockey League team.

Joining Mikita for the on-ice ceremony were his wife, Jill, their four children—Meg, Scott, Jane, and Christopher—along with Joe, the uncle who adopted Stan and brought him to St. Catharines, Ontario, at the age of eight from his native Czechoslovakia. Mikita received a two-minute standing ovation when introduced, then another roar of approval when he donned the No. 21 jersey for one last time.

Mikita thanked former coaches Rudy Pilous and Billy Reay; Tommy Ivan, the Blackhawks' longtime general manager; and the Wirtz family that owns the team "for giving us our daily bread." He also saluted his teammates. "Over the 21 years I skated on this pond," he said, "I played with 170 of them. But I really only had five linemates—Kenny Wharram, Ab McDonald, and Doug Mohns from the days of the Scooter Line and, I'm extremely proud to say, that I also played with a couple of plowhorses, Cliff Koroll and John Marks."

Turning to Joe, whom Mikita has referred to as his father since childhood, he said, "I have one more duty that comes from the heart. I'd like to pay tribute to someone who besides giving me love and affection gave me the greatest commodity in life. He took me out of a Communist country and gave me something I think we're all striving for. He gave me my freedom. I'd like to pay tribute to the greatest guy I know. My pop."

Mikita played 1,394 regular season games for the Blackhawks, the most in franchise history, and scored 541 goals, second only to Bobby Hull. He also registered a team-record 926 assists. In 155 playoff games, he amassed 91 assists—both franchise highs—and 59 goals for 150 points, also a Blackhawks record.

Mikita earned the Art Ross Trophy as leading scorer in the NHL four times—1964, 1965, 1967, 1968—the Hart Trophy as most valuable player in 1967 and 1968, and the Lady Byng trophy in 1967 and 1968. He is the only player in NHL annals to win all three of those trophies in the same season. He also won the 1976 Lester Patrick Trophy for contributions to hockey in the United States. He was a first-team NHL All-Star six times and a second-team All-Star twice. Mikita served as team captain from 1975 through 1977.

Bill Wirtz, the team president, hailed Mikita as "the finest player in the history of the Blackhawks franchise." But Mikita said he did not view himself as a superstar. "I'd just as soon be remembered as an athlete who was part of the community," he said. "Chicago, after all, is my home."

—Bob Verdi

ACKNOWLEDGMENTS

We would like to express our gratitude to all involved in making *Forever a Blackhawk* a reality.

Bob Verdi, who is a wizard with words and a joy to work with.

Our family, friends, and the fans, whose input made this book possible. The Chicago Blackhawks organization, Rocky Wirtz, John McDonough, and Jay Blunk, who shocked Bobby Hull and Stan by commissioning statues in their honor. Omri, Julie, and Itamar Amrany and all the incredible artists who took a slab of clay and created an intricate and remarkable likeness of Stan. Finally, Mitch Rogatz, Adam Motin, and all the hardworking people at Triumph Books.

The story of the young boy from humble beginnings who became a chippy hockey player as well as a man who exceeded all his expectations is complete, but *Forever a Blackhawk* will live on through the amazing statue.

—Jill and Stan Mikita